UNITED STATES DEPARTMENT OF THE INTERIOR
Harold L. Ickes, Secretary

GEOLOGICAL SURVEY
W. C. Mendenhall, Director

Bulletin 849—B

LODE DEPOSITS OF THE FAIRBANKS DISTRICT, ALASKA

BY

JAMES M. HILL

Investigations in Alaska Railroad belt, 1931
(Pages 29–163)

UNITED STATES
GOVERNMENT PRINTING OFFICE
WASHINGTON : 1933

For sale by the Superintendent of Documents, Washington, D.C. - - - - - - - Price 35 cents

CONTENTS

ILLUSTRATIONS

INVESTIGATIONS IN ALASKA RAILROAD BELT, 1931

FOREWORD

By Philip S. Smith

To help the mining industry of Alaska and to assist in the development of the mineral resources of the Territory have been the prime motives of the Geological Survey's investigations in Alaska during the past 35 years, in which nearly one half of the Territory has been covered by its reconnaissance and exploratory surveys. It was natural, therefore, that the Alaska Railroad, when it undertook intensive consideration of the problem of finding tonnage that would increase its revenues, should look to the Geological Survey to supply technical information as to the known mineral deposits along its route and to indicate what might be done to stimulate a larger production of minerals and induce further mining developments and prospecting that would utilize its service. Realization of the need for this information had long been felt by the officials responsible for the operation of the Alaska Railroad, and the need had been partly supplied by the Geological Survey, but funds to carry through an extensive inquiry of this sort had not been available until 1930, when a special committee of the Senate, composed of Senators Howell, Kendrick, and Thomas, visited Alaska, studied some of the railroad's problems, and successfully urged Congress to grant it $250,000 for investigations of this kind.

On the invitation of the Alaska Railroad the Geological Survey prepared various plans and estimates for the investigations that appeared to be most likely to contribute the desired information as to the mineral resources. Selection of the problems to be attacked proved difficult, because the choice necessarily was hedged about with many practical restrictions. For instance, each project recommended must give promise of disclosing valuable deposits—a requirement that was impossible to satisfy fully in advance, as it involved prophecy as to the unknown and undeveloped resources. Then, too, it was desirable that the search should be directed mainly toward disclosing deposits which if found would attract private enterprises to undertake their development in the near future. Finally, some of the deposits that might be worked profitably did not appear likely to afford much tonnage to be hauled by the railroad. Under these limitations it should be evident that the projects that could be recommended as worth undertaking with the funds available by no means exhausted the mineral investigations that otherwise would be well justified. In a large sense, all of Alaska may properly be regarded as indirectly contributory to the welfare of the railroad, but even in that part of Alaska contiguous to its tracks there are large stretches of country that are entirely unexplored and large areas that have had only the most cursory examination. Although areas of this sort might well repay investigation, they were excluded from the list of projects recommended because they were not known to contain mineral deposits of value, and it therefore seemed better to make the selection from other areas that had been proved to hold promise. Furthermore, several areas within the railroad zone were excluded because their value was believed to lie mostly in their prospective placers, which would not yield much outgoing tonnage; others because their lodes carried mainly base metals, for which development and the recovery of their metallic content in a readily salable condition were relatively expensive; and still others because their resources consisted mainly of granite, building stone, or some other product for which at present there is only a small local demand.

After careful consideration ten projects were selected, and the funds required for undertaking them were made available. The projects that were selected involved the examination of two areas principally valuable for their coal (Anthracite Ridge and Moose Creek), five areas likely to be principally valuable for gold (Fairbanks, Willow Creek, Girdwood, Moose Pass, and Valdez Creek), and three areas whose lodes consisted mainly of mixed sulphides (the Eureka area in the Kantishna district, Mount Eielson, formerly known as Copper Mountain, and the head of West Fork of Chulitna River). The general position of these different areas is indicated on the accompanying diagram (fig. 1). A general study of the non-metalliferous resources of the entire region traversed by the railroad was included in the projects to be undertaken, but the results obtained were not such as to permit adequate determination of their extent at this time.

Examinations were made in the field in each of the selected areas, all the known prospects and mines being critically examined and sampled so far as time and other conditions permitted. The records thus obtained, together with all other information bearing on the problems, were then subjected to further study in the laboratory and office, in the course of which other Geological Survey specialists whose knowledge and experience could be of assistance were freely consulted. The outcome of all these lines of analysis has been the reports which make up this volume. Although each chapter is presented as embodying the latest and most authoritative information available regarding the districts and properties described up to the time field work in them

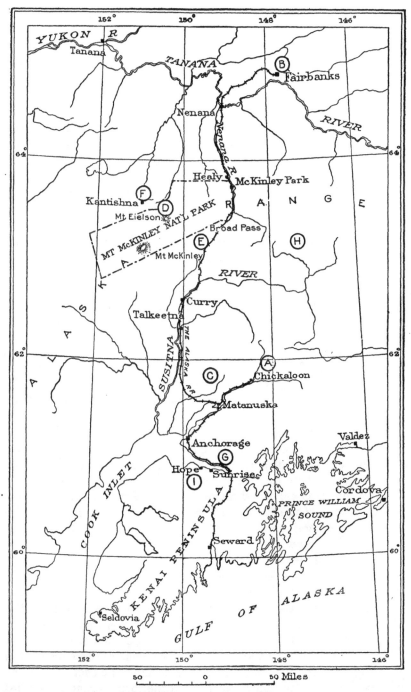

FIGURE 1.—Index map showing areas investigated in Alaska Railroad belt, 1931. A, Anthracite Ridge B, Fairbanks; C, Willow Creek; D, Mount Eielson; E, West Fork of Chulitna River; F, Eureka and vicinity; G, Girdwood; H, Valdez Creek; I, Moose Pass and Hope

was finished, the authors make no claim that all the results they have presented are to be regarded as final nor as solving all the problems that have arisen. Actually none of the mines have been developed to such an extent as to furnish all of the evidence desired to solve the problems involved. At none of the properties is any considerable quantity of ore actually "blocked out" in the engineering sense of that term, so that instead of specific measurements as to the quantity and grade of ore the different camps will yield, the Survey geologists and engineers have necessarily had to make numerous assumptions and be content with estimates and generalizations as to the potential resources. Furthermore, the work was planned so as not to invade the proper field of the private mining engineer in the valuation of individual properties, but rather to occupy the open field of considering the districts as a whole.

In two of the districts, Anthracite Ridge and Moose Creek, whose value lay in their prospective coal resources, the examinations that could be made by ordinary geologic means were not adequate to arrive at a final judgment of the resources of the area but pointed to the desirability of further tests by drilling. As a consequence additional exploration of these districts by means of diamond drilling was authorized, and this work was undertaken in the season of 1932. The results of these tests were not available at the time the manuscripts of the other reports were completed, and rather than delay their publication until the later reports could be finished and incorporated in the volume these reports have been omitted here and will be published later elsewhere.

This is not the place to summarize the detailed findings of the geologists as to the merits of the different districts, as those findings are explained in detail and summarized in the respective chapters. Suffice it to say here that on the whole the principal purpose of the investigations was carried through satisfactorily and that while the studies in some of the districts indicate that they hold little promise of extensive mineral development in the near future, others appear to encourage development under existing conditions, and still others seem to be worth development when some of the existing factors such as transportation or price of base metals are improved. That conditions which are now temporarily retarding the development of some of the deposits will become more favorable cannot be doubted. The entire region is becoming more accessible each year, and as a result costs are being lowered and experience is being gained as to the habit of the various types of deposits, so that the conclusions expressed in this volume as to the resources of the different districts should be reviewed from time to time in the light of the then current conditions.

LODE DEPOSITS OF THE FAIRBANKS DISTRICT

By James M. Hill

OUTLINE OF REPORT

The Fairbanks district is underlain by pre-Cambrian metamorphic schists of sedimentary origin having a considerable range in composition. The schists are overlain by extensive gold-bearing gravel and muck in the valleys, and natural exposures on the hillsides and even on the summits are extremely rare, because of the heavy cover of moss and bushes. The cleavage of the schists has a general well-defined structural trend, which in the eastern part of the district, or Pedro Dome area, strikes about east and dips 15° to 45° both north and south. In the western part of the area, in the vicinity of Ester Dome, the trend is slightly east of north, and this has influenced both intrusion and mineralization in that area.

The schists have been intruded by igneous rocks of several types. The earliest is a fine-grained quartz diorite, which is well exposed on Pedro Dome. The diorite was followed by a coarse-grained biotite granite porphyry and this by finer-grained quartz porphyry, which in some dikes is represented by aplitic rock. These intrusive rocks occur in two principal areas as elongated nearly parallel bodies following the general structural trend, one north and one south of the Goldstream Valley northeast of Fairbanks. There are probably a large number of small offshoots or dikes from these large masses, but the deep surface cover has obscured most of them, and only a few of them have been traced and mapped. Ester Dome has relatively little igneous rock in the more highly mineralized area on its southeast side, but a few small outcrops of these rocks show that the dikes follow the northward-trending structure.

The principal mineral deposits of economic interest, aside from the extensive gold placers, are the gold quartz veins, from a few inches to 15 feet wide. Many of these veins carry from 1½ to 2 percent of sulphides and free gold. The principal sulphides are arsenopyrite and stibnite, but galena, jamesonite, sphalerite, and löllingite have been recognized. The gold accompanied the sulphides in part and was deposited in a third stage of reopening of the veins. Adequate evidence is available to show that the gold is largely primary and that the tenor of ore probably will not change with depth to any appreciable amount. Much of the gold is free, so that a large part of it may be recovered from the ore by simple metallurgical treatment. Economic conditions, though presenting some difficulties, are much superior to those in many other mining camps in northern latitudes, for transportation is available throughout the year, and the camp is not isolated.

In 1931 there were nearly 100 gold-lode properties at which sufficient work had been done to allow some measure of examination. At about 40 of these prospecting and development were under way, and 10 properties were producing. A considerable amount of underground development has been done at the Ready Bullion, Billy Sunday, Ryan, and Mohawk mines, on Ester Dome, and at the Newsboy, Cleary Hill, Tolovana, Wyoming, and Hi-Yu properties, in the Pedro Dome area. The deepest development in the district had reached 350 feet below the surface, but in 1931 no workings below a depth of 250 feet were open for inspection.

The Fairbanks district produced nearly $80,000,000 from placer deposits in the years 1904 to 1930. It is estimated that dredges or other mechanical devices, reworking the same streams and others that could not be worked by hand methods, may produce an even greater amount during the next 25 years. It is believed that the lode gold deposits, which produced nearly $2,000,000 from 1910 to 1930, if mined with adequate financial support and skilled technical and administrative direction, can produce in the next 25 years an amount of gold that will compare favorably with that so far yielded by the placer deposits.

Deposits of stibnite also occur in the Fairbanks district and were worked in the past when high prices for antimony prevailed. It is by no means unlikely that they may be mined again if prices reach a sufficiently high level. The antimony ores occur in the gold lodes but usually as minor deposits formed by segregation. In a few places stibnite was deposited in these lodes to the practical exclusion of the other sulphides and gold.

The tungsten deposits of the district were mined only under the stimulus of a very high price during the World War, and resumption of mining them in the near future is not regarded as probable, in part because of their small size and low tenor, but in part because of their distance from markets. These deposits are quartz-scheelite veins, which either have replaced small lenticular bodies of limestone or occur as contact-metamorphic deposits in the vicinity of acidic intrusive rocks. They are therefore to be sought in widely separated tracts, but they are likely to be irregular and sparsely disseminated.

INTRODUCTION

EARLY INVESTIGATIONS

The Fairbanks district includes an area of about 300 square miles surrounding the town of Fairbanks, which lies on Chena Slough, a branch of the Tanana River, in latitude 64°51' north and longitude 147°42' west. (See fig. 1.) From the discovery of placer gold in this district, in 1902, and the beginning of extensive placer mining, in 1904, to the end of 1930 the district produced from its placers and lodes nearly $82,000,000 worth of gold and silver, and it still has large reserves of these metals yet to be mined. The district and surrounding regions have been visited at intervals since 1898 by many geologists of the Geological Survey, and the geology, geography, mineral deposits, and water resources have been studied, with the result that a considerable body of information has been published. This information appears in a large number of separate publications, many of which are out of print and no longer obtainable. The following list includes the principal Geological Survey publications that deal with the Fairbanks district and with surrounding parts of the Yukon-Tanana region. Those for which a price is given can be obtained from the Superintendent of Documents, Washington, D.C.; the one marked " **free** " can be obtained on application to the Director of the Geological Survey, Washington, D.C.; the others are out of print but may be found in some of the larger libraries.

The gold placers of the Fortymile, Birch Creek, and Fairbanks regions, by L. M. Prindle. Bulletin 251, 1905, 89 pp.

Yukon placer fields, by L. M. Prindle. In Bulletin 284, 1906, pp. 109–131.

Reconnaissance from Circle to Fort Hamlin, by R. W. Stone. In Bulletin 284, 1906, pp. 128–131.

The Yukon-Tanana region, Alaska: Description of the Circle quadrangle, by L. M. Prindle. Bulletin 295, 1906, 27 pp.

The Bonnifield and Kantishna regions, by L. M. Prindle. In Bulletin 314, 1907, pp. 205–226.

The Circle precinct, Alaska, by A. H. Brooks. In Bulletin 314, 1907, pp. 187–204.

The Yukon-Tanana region, Alaska: Description of the Fairbanks and Rampart quadrangles, by L. M. Prindle, F. L. Hess, and C. C. Covert. Bulletin 337, 1908, 102 pp.

Occurrence of gold in the Yukon-Tanana region, by L. M. Prindle. In Bulletin 345, 1908, pp. 179–186.

The Fortymile gold placer district, by L. M. Prindle. In Bulletin 345, 1908, pp. 187–197.

Water supply of the Fairbanks district in 1907, by C. C. Covert. In Bulletin 345, 1908, pp. 198–205.

Water-supply investigations in Alaska, 1906 and 1907, by F. F. Henshaw and C. C. Covert. Water-Supply Paper 218, 1908, 156 pp.

Water-supply investigations in Yukon-Tanana region, 1907 and 1908, by C. C. Covert and C. E. Ellsworth. Water-Supply Paper 228, 1909, 108 pp.

The Fortymile quadrangle, by L. M. Prindle. Bulletin 375, 1909, 52 pp.

The Fairbanks gold-placer region, by L. M. Prindle and F. J. Katz. In Bulletin 379, 1909, pp. 181–200.

Water supply of the Yukon-Tanana region, 1907 and 1908, by C. C. Covert and C. E. Ellsworth. In Bulletin 379, 1909, pp. 201–228.

Sketch of the geology of the northeastern part of the Fairbanks quadrangle, by L. M. Prindle. In Bulletin 442, 1910, pp. 203–209.

Auriferous quartz veins of the Fairbanks district, by L. M. Prindle. In Bulletin 442, 1910, pp. 210–229.

Placer mining in the Yukon-Tanana region, by C. E. Ellsworth. In Bulletin 442, 1910, pp. 230–245.

Water supply of the Yukon-Tanana region, 1909, by C. E. Ellsworth. In Bulletin 442, 1910, pp. 251–283.

Placer mining in the Yukon-Tanana region, by C. E. Ellsworth and G. L. Parker. In Bulletin 480, 1911, pp. 153–172.

Water supply of the Yukon-Tanana region, 1910, by C. E. Ellsworth and G. L. Parker. In Bulletin 480, 1911, pp. 173–217.

Water supply of the Fairbanks, Salchaket, and Circle districts, by C. E. Ellsworth. In Bulletin 520, 1912, pp. 246–270.

The Bonnifield region, by S. R. Capps. Bulletin 501, 1912, 64 pp. 20 cents.

A geologic reconnaissance of a part of the Rampart quadrangle, by H. M. Eakin. Bulletin 535, 1913, 38 pp. 20 cents.

A geologic reconnaissance of the Fairbanks quadrangle, by L. M. Prindle, F. J. Katz, and P. S. Smith. Bulletin 525, 1913, 220 pp. 55 cents.

A geologic reconnaissance of the Circle quadrangle, by L. M. Prindle. Bulletin 538, 1913, 82 pp. 30 cents.

Lode mining near Fairbanks, by Theodore Chapin. In Bulletin 592, 1914, pp. 321–356.

Surface water supply of the Yukon-Tanana region, by C. E. Ellsworth and R. W. Davenport. Water-Supply Paper 342, 1915, 343 pp. 45 cents.

The Yukon-Koyukuk region, by H. M. Eakin. Bulletin 631, 1916, 88 pp. 20 cents.

The gold placers of the Tolovana district, by J. B. Mertie, Jr. In Bulletin 662, 1918, pp. 221–277. 75 cents.

Lode mining in the Fairbanks district, by J. B. Mertie, Jr. In Bulletin 662, 1918, pp. 403–424. 75 cents.

Lode deposits near the Nenana coal field, by R. M. Overbeck. In Bulletin 662, 1918, pp. 351–362. 75 cents.

The Kantishna district, by S. R. Capps. Bulletin 687, 1919, 118 pp. 25 cents.

The Nenana coal field, Alaska, by G. C. Martin. Bulletin 664, 119, 54 pp. $1.10.

The occurrence of metalliferous deposits in the Yukon and Kuskokwim regions, by J. B. Mertie, Jr. In Bulletin 739, 1922, pp. 149–165. 25 cents.

Mining in the Fortymile district, by J. B. Mertie, Jr. In Bulletin 813, 1930, pp. 125–142.

Geology of the Eagle-Circle district, by J. B. Mertie, Jr. Bulletin 816, 1930, 168 pp. 50 cents.

Mining in the Circle district, by J. B. Mertie, Jr. In Bulletin 824, 1931, pp. 155–172, 1932. 20 cents.

A geologic reconnaissance of the Dennison Fork district, by J. B. Mertie, Jr. Bulletin 827, 1932, 44 pp. 45 cents.

The Tatonduk-Nation district, Alaska, by J. B. Mertie, Jr. In Bulletin 836, 1932, pp. 347–443. 75 cents.

The following is a list of the published maps:

Circle quadrangle, scale 1:250,000; by T. G. Gerdine, D. C. Witherspoon, and others. In Bulletin 295, 1906.

Fairbanks quadrangle, scale 1:250,000; by T. G. Gerdine, D. C. Witherspoon, R. B. Oliver, and J. W. Bagley. In Bulletin 337, 1908.

Fortymile quadrangle, scale 1:250,000; by E. C. Barnard. In Bulletin 375, 1909.

Rampart quadrangle, scale 1:250,000; by D. C. Witherspoon and R. B. Oliver. In Bulletin 337, 1908.

Circle quadrangle (no. 641), scale 1:250,000; by T. G. Gerdine, D. C. Witherspoon, and others. 1911. 50 cents retail or 30 cents wholesale. Also in Bulletin 538, 1913, 20 cents.

Fairbanks quadrangle (no. 642), scale 1:250,000; by T. G. Gerdine, D. C. Witherspoon, R. B. Oliver, and J. W. Bagley. 1911. 50 cents retail or 30 cents wholesale. Also in Bulletin 337, 1908, 25 cents, and Bulletin 525, 1913, 55 cents.

Fortymile quadrangle (no. 640), scale 1:250,000; by E. C. Barnard. 1902. 10 cents retail or 6 cents wholesale. Also in Bulletin 375, 1909, 30 cents.

Rampart quadrangle (no. 643), scale 1:250,000; by D. C. Witherspoon and R. B. Oliver. 1913. 20 cents retail or 12 cents wholesale. Also in Bulletin 337, 1908, 25 cents, and part in Bulletin 535, 1913, 20 cents.

Fairbanks special (no. 642A), scale 1:62,500; by T. G. Gerdine and R. H. Sargent. 1908. 20 cents retail or 12 cents wholesale. Also in Bulletin 525, 1913, 55 cents.

Bonnifield region, scale 1:250,000; by J. W. Bagley, D. C. Witherspoon, and C. E. Griffin. In Bulletin 501, 1912, 20 cents. Not issued separately.

Yukon-Koyukuk region, scale 1 : 500,000; by H. M. Eakin. In Bulletin 631, 1916, 20 cents. Not issued separately.

Upper Tanana Valley region, scale 1 : 250,000; by D. C. Witherspoon and J. W. Bagley (preliminary edition). 1922. Free on application.

PRESENT REPORT

The present investigation was undertaken as one of the projects under a special appropriation to the Alaska Railroad for a study of such mineral deposits in the railroad belt as were likely to yield tonnage to the railroad. It was to be confined solely to the lode deposits of the Fairbanks district, the gold placers of the district having long been the object of close attention. The lodes had by no means, however, been neglected by the Geological Survey. The most comprehensive study of the lodes that had been made was that by Smith,[1] in 1912, and later studies were carried out by Chapin,[2] in 1913, and by Mertie,[3] in 1916. Since that time yearly reports on the progress of lode mining there have been issued.

In the present study an attempt was made to determine the amount of ore blocked out and the amount probably recoverable, and samples were taken for assay to determine ore values and to check the results obtained by private sampling. In most of the lode mines of this district mining operations have not been developed far in advance of the mill requirements, so that there are few large reserves of ore blocked out in an engineering sense. Nevertheless, it was in many places possible to predict with some confidence the probable ore reserves and to make conservative estimates of the ore resources of particular mines. This has been done with a full realization that not all the figures given can be supported by actual measurements of ore developed on three sides but they represent the writer's judgment of the probabilities.

The writer arrived in Fairbanks June 7, 1931, to undertake the study whose results are here presented, and ended his field work September 15. During that period he visited all the lode mines and prospects of which he could obtain any information and made a study of the general geology insofar as it had a bearing on the problems of ore deposition. Many mines and prospects on which active work has been carried out in the past have become inactive, and the openings, both surface and underground, have caved so that they are no longer accessible. A few of these were cleaned out for the purposes of this study, but many of them were so badly caved or of so

[1] Prindle, L. M., Katz, F. J., and Smith, P. S., A geologic reconnaissance of the Fairbanks quadrangle, Alaska: U.S. Geol. Survey Bull. 525, pp. 153–216, 1913.

[2] Chapin, Theodore, Lode mining near Fairbanks: U.S. Geol. Survey Bull. 592, pp. 321–355, 1914.

[3] Mertie, J. B., Jr., Lode mining in the Fairbanks district: U.S. Geol. Survey Bull. 662, pp. 403–424, 1918.

little importance that their reopening was not justified. For those the descriptions published by earlier workers are here quoted or abstracted. In his discussion of the geography and geology and description of mines the writer has drawn copiously from the writings of earlier Geological Survey workers in this field. For the sake of brevity their statements have in many places been abstracted, without making reference to the reports from which the information was drawn. A few of the pertinent facts of the general geology that had a bearing on the writer's special problems are summarized, but the general geology of the region has been adequately treated in earlier reports, especially Bulletin 525, and no attempt is made to duplicate that discussion.

ACKNOWLEDGMENTS

The writer is greatly indebted to a large number of persons in Fairbanks for favors of various kinds. He was ably assisted in the field by William McConn. The officers of the Fairbanks Exploration Co., including O. J. Egleston, J. D. Harlan, and R. B. Earling, were particularly gracious in permitting the use of their office facilities and in supplying data and maps of great value. Likewise President Bunnell and Dean E. N. Patty, of the Alaska Agricultural College and School of Mines, gave fullest cooperation. Dean Patty supplied maps of nearly all the mine workings in the district, either from his private collection or from reports made by students. In this way late maps were obtained of all the important development work on Ester Dome from the thesis of Robert McCombe and Grant Augustine, Jr. Paul Hopkins, of the United States Bureau of Mines, made a large number of assays and was of great assistance in many ways. Lynn Smith, United States marshal, and Thomas Hunt, receiver of the United States Land Office, gave much help.

Of the mining men of the district particular thanks are due to Messrs. Stroecker and Wesch, of the First National Bank; Mr. Bericke, of the Samson Hardware Co.; E. A. Smith, of Smith Bros. Hardware Co.; Martin Pinska, Pietro Vigna, M. E. Stevens, A. A. Zimmerman, and the Gustafson Bros., of Cleary Hill Mines; William McCarthy, Harry Feldmann, and E. A. Austin, of Fairbanks Creek; and Sam Godfrey, of the Beaver Creek Dredging Co. J. Henderson, Samuel Stay, William McConn, Mr. Stevens, Mr. Borovich, and J. McDonald were of great assistance in the study of Ester Dome. In the office, C. P. Ross, C. F. Park, and D. F. Hewett gave help in the study of thin sections and polished specimens.

GEOGRAPHY

POSITION AND EXTENT

The Fairbanks district lies within the Yukon-Tanana region, which forms the central plateau Province of Alaska. This dissected plateau is diversified by many broad valleys and their smaller tributaries and is characterized by broad, rolling interstream areas from which rise numerous rounded domes and some rather large mountain masses. The surface of the upland maintains remarkable uniformity of elevation throughout considerable areas. It stands 3,000 to 3,500 feet above sea level in the eastern part of the region, gradually falls off westward to the vicinity of Fairbanks, where it is only about 2,000 feet in elevation, and rises again to 3,000 feet near the Yukon at Rampart.

The domes, which rise above the general level of the upland, are irregularly distributed and attain elevations of 4,000 to 5,000 feet. Some of them are composed of stocks of igneous rock, and some are made up of closely folded sediments, but in both types the relief is due to the greater resistance to erosion of the constituent rocks.

This great dissected plateau region is drained by two large rivers, the Yukon on the north, and its principal tributary, the Tanana, on the south.

The town of Fairbanks is situated on Chena Slough, a channel of the Tanana River that in medium stages of water is navigable by shallow-draft river boats up to the town. The Fairbanks district, as that term is here used, includes an area of about 550 square miles, mostly northeast of Fairbanks. (See pl. 3.) The district is drained on the northwest by the Chatanika River and its tributaries; its central part includes the basin of Goldstream Creek, a tributary of the Chatanika; and the district includes also the headward portions of a few creek basins that drain southward to the Tanana.

A more complete description of the geography of the Yukon-Tanana region and of the Fairbanks district has already been published.[4]

CLIMATE

GENERAL CONDITIONS

The climate, although influenced by the position of the Fairbanks quadrangle in the interior of Alaska, far from the coast line, and by its elevation above sea level, owes its most striking characteristics to the high latitude. The snowfall is not large, but during the long, intensely cold winters the circulation of water is reduced to a minimum. Throughout much of the region the ground is frozen to great depths, alluvial deposits having been reported to be frozen for more than 300 feet below the surface. Differences in material, however, and in the position of the material with reference to drainage have to some extent governed the distribution of frozen ground, and considerable areas of alluvial deposits are unfrozen.

---

[4] Prindle, L. M., Katz, F. J., and Smith, P. S.. A geologic reconnaissance of the Fairbanks quadrangle, Alaska: U.S. Geol. Survey Bull. 525, 1913.

Notwithstanding the continuance of temperature far below freezing, with ice on the larger streams and lakes to a thickness of 5 or 6 feet, much water circulates, frequently breaking through ice already formed and overflowing, thus thickening the ice by successive accumulations on the surface. On the larger streams such overflows are a source of delay and danger in travel, and on the smaller streams they form great deposits of ice that may linger till late in summer and interfere with mining.

The Yukon and Tanana break up at dates ranging from May 10 to May 15. A few days after the ice breaks the rivers are generally clear of ice.

The conditions in summer are similar to those prevailing in temperate regions except for the longer days and shorter seasons characteristic of northern latitudes.

The available records regarding temperature and precipitation show frosts in June and July, but as a rule killing frosts do not occur in these months. The last killing frosts are likely to occur between May 15 and some date early in June. At Fairbanks the first fall frost comes about August 15, and killing frosts come by the middle of September.

The Fairbanks district is in the eastern portion of the " interior climatic province " discussed by Abbe,[5] after a study of climatic records including the year 1902. Since 1904 complete meteorologic records have been kept at Fairbanks, and these records can be obtained from the United States Weather Bureau.

TEMPERATURE

From May to September the mean temperature does not reach as low as 32° F. at Fairbanks, and in these months there are occasional hot days with maximum temperatures of 95° to 99°. By mid-September colder weather sets in, and from October to February the maximum temperature is not much above freezing. From November to March minimum temperatures of 50° to 60° below zero may occasionally occur. During nearly the entire time from October to April the mean temperature is below freezing, and for over two thirds of the time in December, January, and February the mean temperature is below zero.

PRECIPITATION

The region is semiarid. The average annual precipitation (rain and melted snow), computed from the records up to the end of 1929, is 11.45 inches at Fairbanks. The greatest annual precipitation recorded is 18.73 inches at Fairbanks in 1907, and the smallest 7.73 inches in 1927. The rains are local, are small in amount, rarely measuring as much as 0.5 inch at a time, and are of short duration.

---

[5] Abbe, Cleveland, Jr., in Brooks, A. H., The geography and geology of Alaska: U.S. Geol. Survey Prof. Paper 45, pp. 154 et seq., 1906.

From June to September, particularly in July and August, is the season of heaviest rainfall; from February to April, that of the least. There are about 90 rainy days in the year, of which half occur in June, July, August, and September. Snow may fall in practically any month except June and July, though the greatest snowfall is usually in January. The snowfall is never so heavy as to impede traffic seriously and in some years has been so light as to make sledding difficult.

VEGETATION

Vegetation is abundant throughout the Fairbanks district, its distribution being controlled largely by the elevation. Timber line is approximately 2,500 feet above sea level. As the tops of Pedro and Ester Domes are practically the only points within the Fairbanks district that rise above that elevation, almost the entire district lies within the zone in which trees can grow. However, there are considerable areas below 2,500 feet in which no trees were originally present, and the demands for cordwood for fuel have resulted in the cutting off of large areas that were naturally forested, particularly in the vicinity of the mines. Along the floors of the main valleys there was originally a good stand of spruce timber with many trees as much as 2 feet in diameter, and these could be sawed for lumber, but by far the greater part of the timber, consisting of spruce, birch, poplar, and tamarack, is too small for saw timber and is of use only for mine timbers and lagging and for cordwood.

Aside from the trees mentioned the vegetation consists of mosses and grass, with many bushy plants, including willows, alder, dwarf birch, berry bushes, and other small shrubs.

In spite of the high latitude of the district, farming has been carried on for many years, and a considerable number of persons make their living from the soil by supplying food crops and dairy products to the local market. A Government agricultural station has long been in successful operation near Fairbanks, and strains of both plants and livestock that are hardy in that climate have been developed.

WATER SUPPLY

Water supply has always been a serious factor in mining economics in the Fairbanks district. This is emphasized by the 100-mile ditch that the Fairbanks Exploration Co. built and maintains at considerable expense to supply its dredge operations. The topographic relief is not great, and the topographic maturity of the country has resulted in an intricate drainage pattern. There is not much water in any of the smaller creeks, and the small gulches are dry for the most part. The region being semiarid, it is not surprising that springs are few, and many of these occur along the major deeper drainage lines. Most of the quartz mills have been able to get small but adequate supplies of water for summer use by building short ditches or pipe lines. Mill water for winter operation has to be pumped from wells inside the mill buildings to prevent freezing in the extremely long cold season, and this scarcity of water for winter milling is one of the serious problems that must be faced by those who contemplate year-round operations.

There is little chance of developing hydroelectric energy, and it would be of very doubtful economic feasibility because of the cheapness of Nenana coal. This coal is used by the large central steam-electric power plant of the Fairbanks Exploration Co. just north of Chena Slough, on the line of the Alaska Railroad.

The volume of discharge of the stream is of major importance in placer-mining operations but is of much less significance to the lode miner. The subject of the water supply of the district has been discussed by Parker.[6]

POPULATION AND LOCAL INDUSTRIES

The town of Fairbanks is the commercial center of the district. Its permanent population numbered 2,500 in 1931. Many smaller settlements earlier established in response to the needs of the placer-mining industry are now practically abandoned. It is probable that the total permanent population of the district outside of Fairbanks does not exceed 2,500 persons. There is an influx each summer of transients, whose number varies with the demands of the mining industry or with the excitement caused by new discoveries of gold.

The sawmills in the Tanana Valley supply part of the local needs for lumber, and the neighboring ranches provide potatoes, vegetables, hay, milk, and eggs. With an excellent local market, competing only with supplies brought in from the States, farming has been reasonably profitable, but its further expansion is dependent on the continued prosperity and growth of the mining industry. Outside of the articles mentioned above, the region supplies nothing but fish, game, and some wild fruits. Fur-bearing animals are too scarce in the immediate vicinity of the mining camps to supply even the local demand.

Fairbanks is an attractive town, built on the flood plain of the Tanana River and provided with all the essentials and many of the luxuries of modern life. It has a bank and newspapers, a movie theater, several hotels, an electric-light plant, and a telephone system that connects with the mining camps of the vicinity. The military telegraph lines and radio keep it in touch with the outside world.

---

[6] Parker, G. L., Water supply of the Fairbanks district: U.S. Geol. Survey Bull. 525, pp. 131–140, 1913.

MEANS OF COMMUNICATION

Freight from Pacific coast ports in the United States reaches Fairbanks over the Alaska Railroad from Seward, an ice-free port at the head of Resurrection Bay. This port is served by passenger and freight vessels operating out of Seattle, Wash., at frequent intervals throughout the year, as well as by freight steamers whose calls are more or less irregular. Passenger rates on the steamers from Seattle to Seward are from $70 up for first-class accommodations. The railroad fare from Seward to Fairbanks is $47.05, to which must be added the expenses for an overnight stop at the railroad-operated hotel at Curry. Freight rates are discussed under " Economic factors affecting mining " on pages 52–54.

Express for Fairbanks is sometimes taken from the boats at Valdez and brought in by trucks over the Richardson Highway, a distance of about 370 miles. The freight trucks from Valdez make the trip in about 20 hours' running time.

Passengers will also find airplanes available at either Valdez or Seward that can make the flight to Fairbanks in about 5 hours under favorable weather conditions. There are four airplane companies having bases at the well-equipped and efficiently manned Eielson Airport at Fairbanks—the Alaska Airways, Inc., Pacific International Airways, Northern Air Transport Co., and Gillam Airways. There are published tariffs between points on scheduled routes of flight, and flat-rate charges of about $75 an hour of flying time from base to base, to any destination where landing areas are available. Alaskans are air-minded, and it is no unusual thing for the prospector or trapper to take a plane to his remote camp, thereby saving days if not weeks of weary travel on foot or by boat. As pointed out by Governor Parks,[7]

The commercial success and progress of aviation in the Territory has far exceeded the expectations of the most optimistic persons interested in its advancement. The economic benefits resulting from this new method of transportation in fostering Territorial development cannot be easily overestimated, and every possible encouragement and aid by both the Federal Government and Territory should be rendered.

Roads are available for local transportation to the various parts of the Fairbanks district. The Steese Highway, from Fairbanks to Circle, on the Yukon, passes northeastward through the Goldstream and Cleary Creek Valleys, along which are located many of the larger lode mines of the camp. From Summit House, 20 miles northeast of Fairbanks, branch roads lead to Fairbanks Creek, Fish Creek, and Little Eldorado Creek. From Fox, 12 miles northeast of Fairbanks,

---

[7] Parks, G. A., Annual report of the governor of Alaska to the Secretary of the Interior for 1930, p. 39, 1930.

a branch road goes north up Fox Gulch and down the ridge to Dome Creek and Olnes. In the fall of 1931 a right of way northward from Olnes to the Livengood district was being cleared.

. The Ester Dome section, 12 miles west of Fairbanks, is served by a good gravel highway with numerous branches to the more fully developed mines and prospects.

Automobiles are used for all local transport of both persons and supplies. A large number of private cars are owned in Fairbanks, and there are cars for hire at reasonable rates. The Fairbanks Exploration Co., the largest user of transportation in the district, maintains a considerable fleet of passenger and light trucks, as well as several heavy-duty trucks. The cost of transportation by freight trucks is discussed on page 54.

For very heavy hauling and for use in parts of the area where there are no roads the caterpillar tractor has been found most efficient, and there are many of them available for hire at $25 to $50 a day, the price depending on the location and type of work to be done.

Central Alaska, in which the Fairbanks district is located, is served by an excellent wireless telegraph service, manned and maintained by the United States Army. There is also a local telephone line which has exchange agreements with the Government-owned telephone line of the Alaska Railroad.

During the summer of 1931 mail arrived at Fairbanks from the "outside" once a week, ordinarily reaching town each Saturday afternoon. There are local star-route mail and passenger busses between Fairbanks and Berry, on Ester Creek, and Cleary and Chatanika, on Cleary Creek.

GEOLOGY

GENERAL FEATURES

The Fairbanks district lies in an area in which with very minor exceptions all the rocks are either pre-Cambrian schists or Mesozoic intrusives in the schists. (See pl. 3.)

The geology of this area was studied in detail in the years 1903 to 1909 by L. M. Prindle and F. J. Katz, and the mines of the region were examined in 1912 by P. S. Smith. The results of their work were published as Bulletin 525 in 1913. Geologists of the Alaskan branch of the Geological Survey have visited the Fairbanks district almost yearly since 1913 and contributed to the knowledge of the geology and mine operations of the district. However, except for very minor changes in outline of rock areas the geologic map by Prindle, Katz, and Smith published in 1913 is excellent.

It was not the purpose of the present investigation to reexamine in detail the geology of the area, so that in the main the geologic statements are based primarily on the earlier studies.

The geologic map (pl. 3), on a scale of about a mile to the inch, shows the distribution of the more important geologic units. Two types of the Birch Creek schist are mapped, one including the schist proper and the other the crystalline limestone. The unmetamorphosed sedimentary rocks shown include Quaternary and some Tertiary beds, the former being represented by terrace and present stream deposits. The igneous rocks mapped are augen gneiss, probably of pre-Cambrian age, quartz diorite intrusives, porphyritic granite intrusives, altered dike rocks, and basalts.

STRATIGRAPHY

PRE-CAMBRIAN ROCKS (BIRCH CREEK SCHIST)

CHARACTER

The metamorphic rocks classed as Birch Creek schist form by far the greatest part of the visible bedrock of the district. The latest definition and description of the Birch Creek schist, and the one now accepted by the Geological Survey, is that given by Mertie.[8] He describes the character, structure, thickness, age, correlation, and the petrographic character of this formation in considerable detail, so that only a brief summary of the salient characters of this formation is given here.

The Birch Creek schist includes all the pre-Cambrian sedimentary rocks of the Yukon-Tanana region. In this metamorphic assemblage there are some schists of igneous origin that have not been separated on the geologic map, but these are not considered a part of the Birch Creek schist. It is expected that the rocks now included in the Birch Creek schist will eventually be subdivided when more detailed work is done.

Most of the rocks of the Birch Creek schist are either schistose or gneissoid. They include quartzite, quartzite schist, quartz-mica schist, mica schist, graphite schist, crystalline limestone, and calcareous schist. The associated metamorphic igneous rocks include granitic and dioritic gneiss, amphibolite, hornblende schist, and some sericite and chlorite schists. Nearly all of these rocks are recrystallized, but in some of them traces of the original sedimentary or igneous fabric can still be seen.

Among the schistose rocks quartzite schist is perhaps the most common, followed closely by quartz-mica schist, quartzite, and mica schist. The quartzite schist and quartzite occur for the most part in beds 1 foot to several feet thick and weather into blocky talus piles.

Within this district, particularly along the ridges south of the Chatanika River, there are numerous masses of crystalline lime-

8 Mertie, J. B., Jr., Geology of the Eagle-Circle district, Alaska: U.S. Geol. Survey Bull. 816, pp. 13–20, 1930.

stone associated with hornblende and quartzite schists. The limestone is generally thin-bedded, occurring as thin calcareous bands in schist, and ranges in color from white to rather dark bluish gray. Locally it contains tremolite, epidote, and garnet. Elsewhere the limestones are silicated and contain abundant garnet, pyroxene, amphibole, and titanium minerals. These rocks are described in considerable detail by Prindle and Katz [9] and are of special interest here because where cut by granitic intrusive rocks they are in places mineralized with scheelite, sphalerite, chalcopyrite, and pyrite.

STRUCTURE

The pre-Cambrian rocks have without doubt been subjected to diastrophism during many different periods. They, therefore, reflect in their present structure the combined effects of repeated open and close folding, faulting, and intrusion. Original bedding planes are in many places obliterated and can rarely be determined except in massive quartzites and quartzite schists.

In addition to regional metamorphism, portions of the pre-Cambrian rocks have undergone intense contact metamorphism caused by granitic intrusives of at least three eras, ranging in age from pre-Cambrian to Tertiary.

AGE

For many years the most accurate age assignment that could be made for the Birch Creek schist was that it was pre-Ordovician. More recent studies by Mertie,[10] however, show these rocks to be definitely of pre-Cambrian age, and he has presented that evidence fully elsewhere.

TERTIARY ROCKS

With the exception of the metamorphosed sediments of the Birch Creek schist the only consolidated sedimentary rocks in the district include certain beds of brown micaceous sandstone and conglomerate, composed predominantly of schist fragments and vein quartz, that occur in a small area on Fourth of July Hill and are unlike any other rocks of the district. These rocks are described by Prindle and Katz,[11] who conclude that they are of Tertiary age and should probably be correlated with the coal-bearing Tertiary beds that are so widely distributed in interior Alaska. These Tertiary beds have no direct bearing on the lode deposits of the Fairbanks district.

IGNEOUS ROCKS

INTRUSIVE ROCKS

The intrusive rocks of the Fairbanks district are of especial significance in the present study, for it is believed that the gold quartz

[9] Prindle, L. M., and Katz, F. J., op. cit. (Bull. 525), pp. 62–64.
[10] Mertie, J. B., Jr., op. cit., pp. 17–20.
[11] Prindle, L. M., and Katz. F. J., op. cit., pp. 66–67.

veins of the district as well as the contact deposits in limestone are genetically related to intrusive masses of granitic type. The distribution of these intrusives is shown on plate 3. They include quartz diorite masses; biotite granite and related dike rocks that are later than the quartz diorite and in places cut it; and granitic and dioritic porphyries. All these rocks are believed to be of Mesozoic age. Their character, distribution, petrography, and age have been discussed at length by Prindle and Katz.[12]

EXTRUSIVE ROCKS

Near the northeastern edge of the district there are two localities of small area in which olivine basalt occurs. This rock is evidently a surface lava flow and represents the only flow rocks within the district. It is probably of Tertiary age and has no bearing on the ore deposits of the region.

ALLUVIAL DEPOSITS

Alluvial deposits are widely distributed in the Fairbanks district, and from them has been taken the placer gold that has made this district one of the important mining camps of the continent. Their general distribution is shown on plate 3. Although in the headward portions of the stream valleys the gold-bearing alluvium may be thin enough to be mined by open-cut methods, the larger and wider valleys are remarkable for the depth of the alluvium, which in places attains a thickness of as much as 300 feet. Much of this alluvium is solidly frozen to the greatest depths reached by mining, though locally there is considerable unfrozen ground in which water circulates. The mining excavations show the alluvium to consist, at most places, of an overlying bed of muck, an intermediate bed of barren gravel, and an underlying bed of gravel containing the gold, which has also penetrated some distance into the cracks and crevices of the bedrock. It is believed that this alluvial gold in each basin has been derived by erosion from the gold lodes of that basin and has been transported no great distance from its bedrock source. The placer deposits of the Fairbanks district have been discussed in detail in many reports of the Geological Survey. The study on which this report is based was confined solely to the lode deposits, and no attempt to discuss the placers is made here.

STRUCTURAL RELATIONS OF LODES

The attempt to bring the different groups of material found in the Fairbanks district into a systematic arrangement approximately expressive of their true relations and geologic history must not be considered final. The data are still too meager to permit more than a general statement.

---

[12] Prindle, L. M., and Katz, F. J., op. cit., pp. 68–74.

The rocks are closely folded. Recumbent minor folds are common, and so far as observed the strata are overturned toward the northwest. In places the folding is so close that the limbs are nearly parallel, and cleavage and bedding planes become also parallel. The dips taken and recorded on the map therefore indicate rather the dip of the predominant structural planes, which may or may not be the dip of the bedding.

It is believed that the surface presented by erosion in the Fairbanks district is not far removed vertically from what was originally the contact plane of the pre-Cambrian schists and the overlying Paleozoic rocks. That contact plane has been regarded as one of unconformity, but the exact relations of the rocks involved have not been observed in this district. The presence of Paleozoic rocks to the northwest and of similar rocks regarded as Paleozoic in the Chena Valley suggests in a broad way an anticlinal structure for the area between the Beaver and Chena Rivers. The presence of a calcareous zone in the Goldstream Valley and the existence of another zone, partly calcareous, parallel with it on the southeast side of Chatanika Valley suggest a lithologic relationship between the two. In the Goldstream zone, associated with the calcareous rocks, there is some carbonaceous schist and schist characterized by amphibole; in the northern zone associated with the calcareous rocks, is some carbonaceous schist and rocks characterized by pyroxene, amphibole, and garnet. Along the strike of the latter zone to the northeast, near the edge of the area, hornfels occurs, and still farther off are fine and coarse quartzites that show but little metamorphism. The structure suggested by the lithology and by the degree of metamorphism and borne out by the dips so far as these are available is that of a major anticlinal area south of the Goldstream Valley and one in the area between the Chatanika Valley and the main ridge. These parallel, partly calcareous zones, both of them interbedded in the schists, are regarded as near the upper portion of the schist series. The different development of ferromagnesian minerals in the two zones may have been due partly to differences in the original material and partly to metamorphism at greater depths imposed by an overthrusting of folds from the southeast, suggested by the minor recumbent folds. The occurrence of less metamorphosed rocks to the northeast in the zone along the northwest side of the ridge suggests a pitch in that direction, with successively younger, less deeply buried strata coming into view.

The cleavage of the rocks in the Ester Dome area suggests a fold whose main axis trends nearly north. The cleavage of the schists on the flanks, except where the rocks are broken by later fractures, which is the rule rather than the exception, has relatively low dips both to the east and west.

The area north of Goldstream Valley, including Pedro Dome, on the contrary, is occupied by a series of highly appressed folds whose axes trend approximately east. A very distinct axis of one of these folds, trending a few degrees north of east, passes just north of Pedro Dome and extends eastward along the north side of Fairbanks Creek. The intrusive quartz diorite of Pedro Dome apparently came up along a break near the crest of this fold, which is not symmetrical, the cleavage of the beds to the south dipping 10°–20° S., while north of and close to the axis the beds dip 30°–50° N.

The structure outlined above is intricately cut by a double series of closely spaced faults, some of which are of considerable magnitude. The major faults in the Ester Dome region have a strike either almost parallel to the axis of the fold (north) or perpendicular to it (east). The main fractures in the Pedro Dome area have easterly trends, and the less conspicuous faults strike nearly north.

Much fracturing along both series of breaks took place before the mineralizing solution came in, for the principal veins of the two areas follow the characteristic structural lines of the district. Thus on Ester Dome practically all the veins strike within a few degrees of north, and near Pedro Dome most of the veins strike east.

Movement has continued along these same lines up to the present time. The original veins were shattered at least three times and probably more and recemented by later mineralization. After the mineralization was complete, movement along both series of zones of weakness continued, as indicated by the widespread displacement of the veins. Faults occur both transverse to and parallel with the veins, but they all conform to the major trends of the original structure.

CONTACT METAMORPHISM AND MINERALIZATION

The contact effects of the intrusive rocks seem to have resulted principally in the production of biotite and andalusite from the more micaceous schists and masses of hornblende, garnet, and epidote rocks from the more calcareous members of the Birch Creek. In three localities—at the head of Pearl Creek, a tributary of Fish Creek; on the divide between First Chance, a tributary of Goldstream, and Steele Creek; and on the ditch line about a mile northwest of Fox—limestone members of the Birch Creek schist carry besides the usual contact-metamorphic lime silicate minerals appreciable quantities of scheelite (calcium tungstate). Near the head of Cleary Creek about three quarters of a mile from the Newsboy Summit a lens of limestone has been altered by contact metamorphism to a mass of heavy lime silicates, with a considerable quantity of massive pyrite, sphalerite, and chalcopyrite. It is noteworthy that this phase of mineralization was apparently slightly earlier than the last period of quartz-vein mineralization.

The gold mineralization of the region was intimately connected with the acidic intrusive rocks. Most of the gold quartz veins are found in the schists near either dikes or the larger stocks of intrusive rock. At the mouth of Skoogy Gulch veins have been traced from granite into the surrounding schists, but in general the igneous rocks, even those of the acidic type, are not highly mineralized and contain few veins and none that have been proved of economic importance. Although the developed veins in the main are relatively near bodies of igneous rock, mineralization has occurred where there is no surface evidence of the presence of intrusives in the immediate vicinity of the veins. This is notably true of the strongly mineralized areas at the head of Fairbanks Creek and on Ester Dome. At the Ester Dome locality there are some relatively inconspicuous outcrops of quartz monzonite porphyry, but no igneous rocks were seen in the rather extensive underground openings.

It appears that the principal control of the localization of mineralization was structural, and as a matter of fact the structure also controlled the position and direction of intrusion of the igneous rocks.

ECONOMIC GEOLOGY

MINERAL RESOURCES AND PRODUCTION

The mineral resources of the Fairbanks quadrangle that have been productive to date on a very large scale are the gold placers, but gold lode deposits near Fairbanks have been productive since 1910, and at intervals some shipments of ore have been made from lodes carrying tungsten and antimony. A little stream tin and rutile have been found in some of the placers but apparently not in commercial quantities. No deposits of nonmetallic minerals, limestone, or building stone are known that are of more than minor local commercial value. Peat deposits are not uncommon, but in view of the extensive coal mines in the Nenana field, 70 miles south of Fairbanks, the peat is not regarded as of commercial importance as a fuel, though experiments have indicated its value as a fertilizer.

The developed gold deposits, both lode and placer, tributary to the town of Fairbanks have yielded large amounts of gold. The following tables present a summary of gold and silver production of this district, which is the most productive area of gold in the interior of Alaska. The quantity of silver in both lode and placer bullion produced in this district is so small as to be of little moment, being only 0.5 percent of the total value of the bullion. Up to the end of 1930 the lode mines are estimated to have produced only 2 percent of the total gold-silver bullion produced in the Fairbanks district. (See fig. 2.)

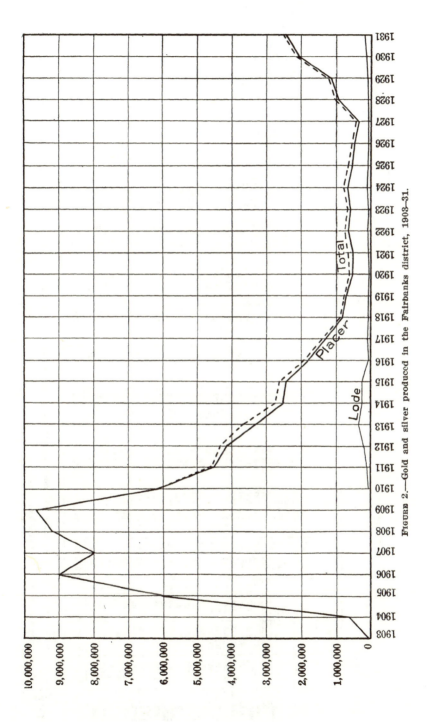

FIGURE 2.—Gold and silver produced in the Fairbanks district, 1903–31.

Gold and silver produced in the Fairbanks district, Alaska, 1903–30

Year	Ore mined (short tons)	Gold recovered						Silver						Combined value of output		
		Lode		Placer		Total		Lode		Placer		Total		Lode	Placer	Combined
		Ounces	Value	Ounces	Value	Ounces	Value a	Ounces	Value	Ounces	Value	Ounces	Value			
1903	148	—	—	1,942	$40,000	1,942	$40,000			348	$188	348	$188		$40,188	$40,188
1904	875	—	—	29,126	600,000	29,126	600,000			5,225	2,821	5,225	2,821		602,821	602,821
1905		—	—	291,262	6,000,000	291,262	6,000,000			52,245	28,212	52,245	28,212		6,028,212	6,028,212
1906		—	—	436,893	9,000,000	436,893	9,000,000			78,367	42,318	78,367	42,318		9,042,318	9,042,318
1907		—	—	388,350	8,000,000	388,350	8,000,000			69,660	37,616	69,660	37,616		8,037,616	8,037,616
1908		—	—	495,146	9,200,000	495,146	9,200,000			79,909	43,151	79,909	43,151		9,243,151	9,243,151
1909		—	—	516,990	9,650,000	516,990	9,650,000			84,027	45,375	84,027	45,375		9,695,375	9,695,375
1910	4,708	841	$17,389	296,116	6,100,000	296,957	6,117,389	106	$57	53,116	28,683	53,222	28,740	$17,446	6,128,683	6,146,129
1911	12,237	3,103	64,145	218,447	4,500,000	221,550	4,564,145	582	308	52,245	27,690	52,827	27,998	64,453	4,527,690	4,592,143
1912	6,626	9,417	194,657	201,456	4,150,000	210,873	4,344,657	1,578	971	48,182	29,632	49,760	30,603	195,628	4,179,632	4,375,260
1913	5,845	16,905	349,457	160,194	3,300,000	177,099	3,649,457	4,123	2,491	20,274	12,245	24,397	14,736	351,948	3,312,245	3,664,193
1914	1,111	10,905	225,421	121,359	2,500,000	132,264	2,725,421	2,209	1,222	29,024	16,050	31,233	17,272	226,643	2,516,050	2,742,693
1915	1,200	10,535	217,776	118,932	2,450,000	129,467	2,667,776	1,796	910	28,444	14,421	30,240	15,331	218,686	2,464,421	2,683,107
1916	1,035	1,905	39,376	87,379	1,800,000	89,284	1,839,376	140	92	11,058	7,276	11,198	7,368	39,468	1,807,276	1,846,744
1917	1,384	2,311	47,781	63,592	1,310,000	65,903	1,357,781	2,217	1,827	8,379	6,904	10,596	8,731	49,608	1,316,904	1,366,512
1918	504	1,294	26,750	38,835	800,000	40,129	826,750	616	616	5,708	5,708	6,324	6,244	27,366	805,708	833,074
1919	944	2,027	41,893	35,437	730,000	37,464	771,893	378	424	5,197	5,820	5,575	6,244	42,317	735,820	778,137
1920	1,724	2,000	20,000	28,155	580,000	29,122	600,000	164	178	3,870	4,218	4,034	4,396	20,178	584,218	604,396
1921	1,270	1,858	38,414	27,670	570,000	29,528	608,414	279	279	3,941	3,941	4,220	4,220	38,693	573,941	612,634
1922	4,528	2,612	54,000	33,641	693,000	36,253	747,000	279	490	b 5,269	4,783	5,548	5,273	54,490	697,783	752,273
1923	3,663	1,191	24,616	29,272	603,000	30,463	627,616	490	246	b 5,942	4,321	6,432	4,567	24,862	607,321	632,183
1924	4,500	4,870	100,673	33,010	c 680,400	37,880	781,073	300	868	b 4,544	3,981	4,844	4,849	101,541	684,381	785,922
1925	6,000	4,064	84,010	25,243	c 520,800	29,307	604,810	1,295	638	b 4,089	3,108	5,384	3,746	84,648	523,908	608,556
1926	5,500	2,467	51,000	22,718	c 468,000	25,185	519,000	919	370	b 3,058	2,552	3,977	2,922	51,370	470,552	521,922
1927		2,467	51,000	16,990	c 350,000	19,457	401,000	590	500	b 8,218	1,734	8,808	2,234	51,500	351,734	403,234
1928	(d)	4,010	82,900	45,655	c 940,500	49,665	1,023,400	880	456	b 8,218	4,808	8,998	5,264	83,356	945,308	1,028,664
1929	(d)	4,013	83,000	55,583	c 1,145,000	59,598	1,228,000	780	525	b 10,005	5,343	10,990	5,868	83,525	1,150,343	1,233,868
1930	(d)	6,483	134,000	135,218	c 2,785,500	141,701	2,919,500	1,585	610	b 24,339	9,371	25,924	9,981	134,610	2,794,871	2,929,481
	70,977	94,247	1,948,258	3,954,611	79,466,200	4,048,858	81,414,458	22,012	14,078	709,466	402,270	731,478	416,348	1,962,336	79,868,470	81,830,806

a Calculated at $20.67 an ounce.
b Quantity of silver based on assumption that average ratio of silver to gold for period was 18 to 82 and that the price of silver for each year was the average as stated in volumes of Mineral Resources.
c Includes smaller placer output of the Richardson district.
d Since 1928 official collection of records of ore mined discontinued owing to indefiniteness as to material to be included.

As will be seen from the table, for many years the ore milled has averaged over $30 a ton. This probably means that at many properties there are reserves of blocked or partly blocked ore carrying less than $30 a ton which could not be mined under the methods of mining and milling in vogue in the past.

At some of the more progressive mines in the district, notably at the Mohawk, on Ester Dome, and the Cleary Hills, Crites & Feldman, and Newsboy, in the Pedro Dome region, costs of operation have been brought down to a point where $10 ore can be worked at a profit. It is the writer's opinion that operating costs can be lowered even more by properly opening the mines and providing adequate milling equipment to make possible greater recovery, as is being done successfully at mines in California where the ores present very similar mining and metallurgical problems.

Scheelite (tungsten-bearing) concentrates from the deposits north of Gilmore Creek and at the head of Pearl Creek, a tributary of Fish Creek, were shipped during the war period of high prices. Over $100,000 worth of high-grade stibnite (antimony) has been shipped from various properties tributary to Fairbanks during the high-price period of the war and also in 1926 and 1927. It is not possible to give exact figures of production of either mineral without divulging confidential information.

The developed gold lode deposits of the Fairbanks district are divided geographically into two groups—one group on Ester Dome and the other in a long, narrow zone trending eastward from the head of Dome Creek, north of Pedro Dome, to the head of Fairbanks Creek, a distance of 8 or 9 miles. This does not mean that other areas are devoid of gold veins but rather that they are scarcely prospected and so far have disclosed no bodies that have tempted development. The developed tungsten deposits all lie along the northern boundary of the large mass of porphyritic granite that forms the divide south of Gilmore Creek. It is believed that scheelite may be found in other places where limestone lenses of the Birch Creek schist are found in close association with acidic intrusive rocks. The antimony deposits are closely associated with the last period of metallization of the gold veins, and pockets or lenses of stibnite may be found in many of the veins and lodes normally worked for gold.

HISTORY OF MINING

As is true in so many gold-mining camps, the discovery and early interest in the Fairbanks district was due to the presence of placer gold in the stream alluvium, the search for the lodes from which the placer gold was derived coming later. Placer gold was first found in the Tanana Valley in the early seventies, though no deposits of commercial importance were then developed. During the next 20 years placers were mined in several tributaries of the Yukon, but the great stimulus to prospecting in the Yukon Basin came in 1896 to 1898, with the discovery of the bonanza placers of the Klondike, when numbers of prospectors spread over that entire region. In 1901 a trading station called Fairbanks was established near the present site of Fairbanks, and the next year placer gold was discovered and claims were staked on Pedro Creek and some of the neighboring streams. When the news of these discoveries became generally known, a stampede to the new-found diggings took place during the winter of 1902–3, but the contrast between the deeply buried placers of this district with the more easily accessible and phenomenally rich placers of the Klondike region dampened the general enthusiasm, and no great impetus to mining resulted from it.

During the summer of 1903 the district developed slowly, but that season's output of about $40,000 demonstrated that paying ground was present, and the next summer rapid development started. It was soon found that throughout much of the district the pay gravel was deeply buried beneath a thick, barren, and mostly frozen overburden. To mine the pay gravel therefore necessitated the use of thawing devices and hoisting machinery and the development of routes of transportation from the navigable rivers to the ground to be mined. The earlier trails thus gave place to wagon roads, and these in turn to a narrow-gage railroad (now abandoned) and finally to the permanent system of excellent automobile roads now being built through the cooperation of the Alaska Road Commission, the Territorial Highway Commission, and the miners.

The development of the town of Fairbanks has kept pace with the development in mining, and minor supply points have come into existence on the most productive creeks.

The early development of the district took place under conditions of very high costs, all heavy supplies being brought in during the summer season of open water by way of the Tanana River. For about 7 months each year the rivers are frozen. More recently, with the completion of the Alaska Railroad from Seward to Fairbanks, opened to traffic in 1924, transportation has been greatly expedited and costs lowered.

During the years that have elapsed since the pioneer days of this camp there has come about the expected change in mining methods. The early mining was done largely by hand or by operations employing only a small number of men and a minimum amount of heavy machinery. With the exhaustion of the bonanza ground, the employment of machinery has increased rapidly, including apparatus for steam and cold water thawing of the frozen ground, hoists and scrapers of various types, and more recently large dredges, which with only a small crew move enormous quantities of material that could not be profitably mined under the old methods.

By the time Fairbanks had become established as an important gold placer camp, the inevitable search for the bedrock source of the gold began. In briefly tracing the history of the development of lode mining in the district the writer is under great obligation to J. D. Harlan, one of the mining engineers of Fairbanks, who had compiled a very complete history of the lode development and who generously offered the use of his manuscript, from which the following statement is largely summarized.

The first quartz claim, the Blue Bell, was located in 1903 on Chatham Creek, but it was not until late in 1908 that much interest was shown in lode prospecting. By 1910, however, veins carrying much gold had been found in Skoogy Gulch and on upper Cleary and Fairbanks Creeks; and it had been shown that a zone of abundant quartz veins extended from Big Eldorado Creek eastward across the heads of Cleary, Willow, Bedrock, and Chatham Creeks to Wolf and Fairbanks Creeks. Pocket-hunting methods were followed, and considerable mining was already in progress.

In 1909 money was raised in Fairbanks by popular subscription to build a 3-stamp mill, and by the end of 1910 about 150 tons of ore averaging $117 to the ton had been milled. At the end of 1911 there were 5 mills in the district, and in that year 875 tons of ore milled yielded $73.66 a ton and 25 or 30 properties were under development.

The production of placer gold in the Fairbanks district declined from $9,650,000 in 1909 to $1,310,000 in 1917. As the placer production began to decline, the people of the district naturally grasped at the hope of sustaining the prosperity of the camp through the development of lode mines. For this reason, no doubt, many lode mines that did not justify development were promoted, financed, and operated for a time. In 1912 over 2,000 lode claims had been staked, and 50 of them had been partly prospected. Six mills had been built and an equal number were under construction. In that year 4,700 tons of ore was milled, yielding an average of $41.55 a ton.

The peak of lode mining was reached in 1913, when more than 12,000 tons of ore was milled, nearly twice the tonnage attained in any other year up to the present time. The decline in 1914 is attributed to a reaction from the enthusiasm that in 1912 and 1913 had led many persons to embark on ill-advised ventures without a proper appreciation of the engineering and economic factors involved.

From 1915 to 1923 lode mining was at a low ebb, the output in none of those years reaching a total of 2,000 tons. It was generally recognized that mining costs were too high, and many projects were postponed pending the completion of the Alaska Railroad.

After the railroad was built, in the summer of 1923, there was a moderate revival in lode mining, and the output has been maintained to the present time at a rate of 2,700 to 6,000 tons of ore a year. The principal producers during recent years have been the Hi-Yu, Mohawk, Rhoads-Hall (later named the Cleary Hill), Wyoming, Tolovana, Henry Ford, Little Eva, and Eva Quartz mines. Considerable prospecting has been done on certain extensive mineralized zones, notably the Ryan lode, on Ester Dome, but no development work has been undertaken on them.

ECONOMIC FACTORS AFFECTING MINING

TRANSPORTATION

The mines of the Fairbanks district are well situated so far as transportation is concerned. Most of them are reached over good to excellent automobile roads leading from the town of Fairbanks, the northern terminus of the Alaska Railroad.

The 470 miles between Seward, the southern coast terminus, and Fairbanks is made in 18 hours actual running time for the mixed passenger and freight train. At present, however, trains are not operated at night, so that an overnight stop is made at Curry, where the Government operates a well-appointed hotel. A train service once a week in each direction is maintained throughout the year, with some extra service during the summer. There are regular freight schedules and such extra freight trains as are required by the traffic.

Passenger fares on the railroad are fixed at the rate of 10 cents a mile, the fare from Seward to Fairbanks being $47.05. Freight rates seem high to one accustomed to rates in the States, but in view of the difficulties of maintenance and operation in this remote region and under such extremes of temperature and precipitation as are found along the Alaska Railroad higher rates than those prevailing in the States are obviously well justified.

The following table gives the freight rates of 1930 and 1931 for certain commodities of particular interest to the mining industry.

Freight rates per ton (2,000 pounds) on certain commodities from Seattle, Wash., to Fairbanks, Alaska, 1930 and 1931

	Ocean rates, Seattle or Tacoma to Seward [a]	Alaska Railroad rates, Seward to Fairbanks		Joint rates, Seattle to Fairbanks	
		1930	1931	1930	1931
Coal, sacked	$5.00	----	[b]$23.80	[b]$25.20	----
Automobiles [c]	----	$54.80	95.00	----	----
General groceries (no high-priced specialties)	----	[b]30.40	[b]47.60	[b]41.00	[b]61.60
Flour and grain products	12.00	16.00	26.40	[b]28.00 / [d]48.60	[b]38.00 / [d]72.00
Hay in bales, 22 pounds or more to a cubic foot	14.50	[b]12.40	[b]19.80	[b]26.80 / [d]57.00	[b]34.00 / [d]83.60
High explosives (powder, etc.)	21.50	[b]54.80 / [d]109.60	[b]95.00 / [d]190.00	[b]75.80 / [d]130.60	[b]116.00 / [d]211.00
Cement	----	[b]17.00	[b]23.80		[b]32.80
Lumber, common, not over 32 feet long	15.00	11.60	[b]18.20	[b]21.60 / [d]49.60	[b]28.00 / [d]72.00
Mining machinery, no single piece over 4,000 pounds	13.00	[b]24.40 / [d]34.60	[b]38.00 / [d]57.00		
Petroleum products	12.50	[b]25.40 / [d]40.00	[b]38.00 / [d]66.60	[b]37.90 / [d]42.50	[b]50.50 / [d]79.10
Return freight southbound (containers, empty drums, etc.), 110 gallons to 24 cubic feet	3.25	[d]17.30	[d]28.50		
Ore and concentrates, value not over $50 a ton [e]	4.50	----	----	[d]18.00 / [f]15.00 / [g]12.00	[d]18.00 / [g]15.00 / [h]12.00

[a] Ton basis for steamship haul is 2,000 pounds or 40 cubic feet, at ship's option.
[b] Carload lots.
[c] Carload lots, minimum 10,000 pounds.
[d] Less than carload lots.
[e] If declared value is more than $50 a ton, 25 percent additional is charged for each $50 or fraction thereof of excess.
[f] Carload lots, minimum 15 tons.
[g] Carload lots, minimum 20 tons.
[h] Carload lots, minimum 10 tons.

Fairbanks is also served during the summer by several passenger busses and regular freight truck lines, operating over the Richardson Highway between Fairbanks and Valdez, a distance of 370 miles, and over the Steese Highway between Fairbanks, Chatanika, and Circle, on the Yukon River, a distance of 160 miles, where connections are made with the up- and down-river boats. There is also a star-route mail bus in operation between Fairbanks and Berry, on Ester Creek 12 miles west.

During 1931 the passenger fare over the Richardson Highway between Fairbanks and Valdez was at times as low as $25, owing to competition, but was usually at least $45. The regular round-trip charge for passengers between Fairbanks and Chatanika, at the mouth of Cleary Creek, is $5. "Drive-yourself" cars can be hired at Fairbanks at $4 to $12 a day, dependent on type of car, length of trip, and character of roads to be driven. Automobiles can be used from April until about the first of the year in the Fairbanks district, but the extremely cold weather of the winter makes driving uncomfortable and somewhat uncertain.

During the summer there is always much trucking in progress, for it is at that time that most of the fuel and heavy supplies are moved from the railroad to the various mines. The rates given below are usual for ordinary hauling contracts. Probably even lower prices could be obtained on long-term regular shipment contracts, though these rates appear to be too low for jobs involving the handling of large pieces of machinery or "special care."

Usual rates per ton for summer trucking in the Fairbanks district

Fairbanks to Chatanika, 30 miles_____ $6.25
Fairbanks to Cleary, 25 miles_____ 5.00
Fairbanks to Fairbanks Creek, 35 miles_____ 7.00
Fairbanks to Ester Dome, 12 miles_____ 4.00

A large part of the very heavy freight, such as large pieces of machinery, mine timber, and hydraulic pipe, which must be moved from localities without improved roads, is moved in winter. Travel in the winter can go in practically any direction, as the surface is frozen and for the most part covered with snow. Caterpillar tractors are extensively used for motive power, and the sizes most commonly used have 30 and 60 horsepower ratings. These machines will haul from 2 to 4 bobsleds, fully loaded, with ease. There are several caterpillars for rent in the district at prices ranging from $40 to $50 a day, which includes driver, bobsleds, fuel, and oil. On work involving long hauls the loaded trains average 20 miles a day. Winter freighting is usually done in March and April, after the severely cold weather has moderated.

LABOR AND WAGES

The Fairbanks district has always been primarily a placer-mining camp, and most of the men who have gone into lode mining are those whose previous mining experience was gained in the placer mines. There are of course, a few notable exceptions, but most of those now engaged in lode mining lack an extensive knowledge of the intricacies of that craft and have had little experience in the mining and timbering of lodes and veins. The labor situation is peculiar in that placer operations afford work for nearly the whole male population during the summer but offer little employment during the remainder of the year. Furthermore, the supply of experienced hard-rock miners is small, and should lode mining in the district be expanded to the extent of its possibilities, more expert quartz miners than are available will be needed.

In 1931 wages for mine labor in the Fairbanks region ranged from $5.25 to $6.50 a day and board, making a total labor charge of

$7 to $8.50 a day, as it is generally agreed that it costs about $2 a day per person to run a suitable camp boarding and bunk house. Although at first these figures seem high, they do not appear unreasonable compared with wages paid in the States (see following table), in view of the factors of climate and costs that must enter into the calculations.

Comparative wage scale, western United States and Alaska

| Type of labor | California | | | Nevada | Alaska |
	Argonaut gold mine [a]	Central Eureka gold mine [b]	Engles copper mine [c]	Nevada-Massachusetts tungsten mine [d]	Alaska-Juneau mine, Juneau [e]
Blacksmith				$6.50	$5.50
Car loader			$4.50		5.00
Chute blaster			5.00		6.00
Hoist man		$5.50	5.00–5.75	5.75–6.00	4.50
Machineman			5.00		5.50
Miner		4.50		5.25	
Miner helper		3.75			4.00
Motorman		5.00	5.00	6.00	
Mucker		3.50	4.50	4.75	5.00
Pipe and trackman			5.00		4.50–5.50
Timberman		4.50	4.50	5.25	5.50
Shift boss	$5.50–6.75		6.00		7.50
Surface labor		3.75			4.70

[a] U.S. Bur. Mines Inf. Circ. 6476, July 1931.
[b] U.S. Bur. Mines Inf. Circ. 6512, October 1931.
[c] U.S. Bur. Mines Inf. Circ. 6260, April 1930.
[d] U.S. Bur. Mines Inf. Circ. 6284, June 1930.
[e] U.S. Bur. Mines Inf. Circ. 6186, October 1929.

TIMBER, LUMBER, AND BUILDING MATERIALS

Cordwood for fuel can be landed in Fairbanks for $10 a cord, and sawmill blocks and slabs can be purchased for a little less.

Ordinary mine timbers can be bought in Fairbanks at about 6 cents a running foot for delivery in Fairbanks. Large timbers with 6 to 10 inch tops and 14 to 18 feet long would cost from 12 to 15 cents a running foot. One contractor sells 17-foot poles with 5 to 6 inch tops delivered at the property for $1 a pole, and poles 16 feet long with 2 to 3 inch tops for lagging at $8.50 a cord of about 90 poles delivered at a mine on Ester Dome.

Owners of mines on Fairbanks and Cleary Creeks pay about $14 to $15 a cord for 16 to 18 foot timbers which average from 2 to 6 inch tops and from which some frame timbers can be cut, though most of the poles delivered in 1931 appeared more suitable for lagging than for posts and caps. Sawed spruce timbers for mill construction at the same points were delivered at $40 to $60 per 1,000 board feet, the price depending on the size and length.

Spruce lumber cut from local timber delivered on a job using 20,000 board feet or more will average $50 per 1,000 board feet, which will include all dimension material. Large selected dimension timber sells for about $80 per 1,000 board feet. Corrugated iron for exterior of mills retails for 10 cents a square foot. Celotex or its equivalent for interior insulation and finishing materials retails for 9 cents and plasterboard for 8 cents a square foot.

POWER

Steam power has been used in the Fairbanks district practically to the exclusion of all other forms of prime movers. Wood fuel was used until rail transportation made coal from the Nenana field available in 1921. A few small gasoline engines, many being old automobile engines, were used to run prospecting hoists and blowers and even mills.

In the spring of 1931 the first semi-Diesel engine at a lode mine in the district was installed to run the Mohawk mill and proved very satisfactory to the owners, as the power cost was cut to nearly one fifth of that incurred when using a coal-fired steam plant. The second installation of the sort was at the Cleary Hill mine, where a 100-horsepower full Diesel engine was installed during the summer of 1931. These plants have demonstrated the great savings in power cost that can be obtained by the use of this type of internal-combustion engines. The writer believes that the Diesel engine will be found to be the most economical power plant for all but the very smallest units.

Coal from the Nenana field was delivered in retail lots in Fairbanks during the summer of 1931 at $8 a ton for mine-run and $9 a ton for lump coal. Lower prices are naturally quoted by the coal producers and dealers for carload orders for delivery at mines, and it was reported that during 1931 mines on Ester Dome were obtaining coal delivered at $6.50 a ton, and on Cleary Creek at $10.50 a ton. No doubt large users of coal who contract directly with the mines for their supply are able to obtain even more favorable prices.

The Standard Oil Co. of California is the only wholesale distributor of petroleum products in the Fairbanks district. Its schedule of prices during the summer of 1931 for delivery at its warehouse was as follows:

Gasoline in drums of 50 gallons or more, 28 cents a gallon.
Diesel oil, gravity 27°. in drums of 50 gallons or more, 22 cents a gallon.
Lubricating oils, in drums:
    Gasoline motor oil, in 5-gallon lots, 90 cents a gallon; in barrel lots, 75 cents a gallon.
    Diesel engine oil, in barrel lots, 80 cents a gallon.

Compressor oil, in 5-gallon lots, 79 cents a gallon; in barrel lots. 74 cents a gallon.

Red engine (bearing) oil, in 5-gallon lots, 60 cents a gallon; in barrel lots, 55 cents a gallon.

Lubricating greases:

Automobile grease, in 50-pound lots, 14.8 cents a pound; in barrel lots, 11.25 cents a pound.

Cup grease, in 50-pound lots, 12.25 cents a pound; in barrel lots, 10.25 cents a pound.

Candles, Miners' Granite, $4.05 a box of 120.

It is understood that on term contracts for considerable quantities of petroleum products a reduction from these prices is given.

MINING SUPPLIES

It is generally supposed by those unfamiliar with Alaska that the cost of supplies is prohibitively high. This may still be true for some of the more isolated mining camps but is not true in the Fairbanks district. As a matter of fact, prices in the retail stores during the summer of 1931 appeared surprisingly low. As a rule they were not as much above prices in the States as the additional handling and freight rates seem to warrant.

Quotations of the prices charged were obtained from the Northern Commercial Co., and the Samson Hardware Co., the two largest dealers in supplies usually associated with mining. The prices quoted were those normally given to mine operators who buy in larger quantities than an individual and presumably represent more nearly jobbing quotations than retail prices. For the sake of comparison with prices in the States the following table includes the wholesale price at Seattle for the same commodities, obtained through the courtesy of the Fairbanks Exploration Co.

No attempt was made to learn the prices asked for foodstuffs and clothing in detail, as these are more personal items. So far as observed the prices quoted on foodstuffs by the chain stores as well as by the individual merchants were practically the same as Seattle prices plus freight and handling charges. Although the price for board in the district is usually assumed to be about $2 per man per day, the mines with large crews are able to cut the price much below that figure.

Prices at Fairbanks and Seattle of a few commodities such as are used in mining, September 1931

Commodity		Fairbanks (jobbing prices)	Seattle (wholesale prices)
Round-point shovels	each	$2.00–$2.25	
	per dozen	24.00–27.00	$18.00
Picks	each	1.50– 2.00	
	per dozen		15.00
⅞-inch drill steel, solid	per pound	.30	.113
Steel rails	per ton	160.00	40.00
⅞-inch steel cable	per foot	.35	.34
	per 100 feet	24.00	
Cement	per ton	55.00	
	per sack	2.75	.80
Carbide	per pound	.15	.06
	per 100 pounds	13.00	
Nails	do	9.00–10.00	2.40
Galvanized iron, corrugated	per square foot	.11	
	per 100 pounds		4.00

HOUSING

In camp construction in the Fairbanks district two conditions not uncommon elsewhere must be met. The most important is the necessity for tight, insulated construction of all houses, including camp, mill, and hoist, to withstand temperatures of 40° to 60° below zero, which will be encountered during the winter. This problem has been faced by many mining companies in various parts of the world and is not difficult of solution. It simply means that camp construction will cost more than in places favored by a milder climate. A second factor to be considered is the necessity for adequate protection of all buildings against insects during the summer. Both of these problems can be met successfully in a number of ways. The methods used in northern Canada have been described in detail with working drawings.[13]

At the Lucky Shot mine, on Craigie Creek, in the Willow Creek district, Alaska, the problem has been well solved by observing the following specifications:

All buildings are covered with double sheeting laid diagonally in opposite directions. Tarred building paper is laid horizontally between this double sheeting. The outside of all buildings is covered with a light-weight composition roofing paper carefully nailed and tarred at all joints. The inside is paneled with insulating board. All buildings are double-windowed, and the main entrances are vestibuled. Floors are double, with building paper between. Finish floors are ⅞ by 4 inch tongue and groove, vertical-grained pine. Heating is done by hot water, piped from the cooling systems of the Diesel engines in the power house. The houses are equipped with concrete-brick chimneys for stoves for auxiliary heating units.

With careful consideration of proper insulation and adequate devices for heating, the housing problem in the Fairbanks district pre-

---

[13] Eng. and Min. Jour., February 16, March 2 and 16, 1929.

sents no features that cannot readily be solved by any builder familiar with a rigorous climate.

METALLURGICAL DATA

It is not the purpose in a report on the geology of the ore deposits of the Fairbanks district to go into a detailed discussion of the metallurgy of the ores. It will be sufficient to point out that similar ores are being handled in California and Oregon and elsewhere in Alaska in relatively simple mills with savings reported to be as high as 95 to 98 percent of the assay values.

Such savings as are shown in the accompanying table are attained only by good planning and close supervision of metallurgical plants. This table gives for comparison the character of ore, type of equipment, mining costs, and metal recovery of six typical mines treating gold ores that include various types of deposits.

Equipment, costs, and metallurgical data of six typical mills treating gold ores

Name and location of mine	Type, character, and size of ore body	Method of gold recovery	Daily capacity of mill	Number of men employed per day (3 shifts)	Type and capacity of coarse-crushing equipment	Type and capacity of fine-grinding equipment
1. Argonaut mine, Jackson, Calif.	Quartz vein in slate and greenstone from 15 to 60 feet wide. 81 percent of gold is free; concentrates pyrite with a little galena, chalcopyrite, and tetrahedrite.	65 percent by amalgamation, 18 percent in concentrates, which are cyanided at custom plant under contract.	300 tons	13 at $4 to $8	35-horsepower jaw-crusher, 16 by 18 inch, break to 2½-inch size.	60 stamps, 1,285 pounds, crush to 24 mesh; 7-inch discharge; 8-inch drop; 5 water to 1 solid.
2. Kirkland Lake Gold mine, Kirkland Lake, Ontario, Canada.	Altered silicified dike rocks, syenite and diabase; auriferous pyrite, possibly tellurides.	Cyanidation. Counter-current decantation all slime.	200 tons	21 at $4.64 to $5.	40-horsepower 12 by 20 inch Buchanan jaw-crusher, to 1½-inch size.	125-horsepower 8 foot by 30 inch Hardinge ball mill, 100-horsepower 5½ by 16 foot tube mill, grinding 96 percent minus 300 mesh.
3. Coniaurum mines, Schumacker, Ontario, Canada.	Quartz and mineralized schist; breaks in slabs up to 10 inches thick.	Cyanidation	500 tons		100-horsepower 10-inch McCully type gyratory, to 1¾-inch size.	62 by 20 inch rolls to ½-inch size; 62 by 20 inch rolls, crush to 67 percent minus 14 mesh and only 12 percent minus 200 mesh; 5 by 16 foot tube mill grinding to 60 percent minus 200 mesh; 35-horsepower per roll.
4. Homestake mine, Lead, S.Dak.	Altered dolomitic limestone in Archean schists containing pyrite, arsenopyrite, and pyrrhotite.	63 percent by amalgamation, 30 percent by cyanidation.	South mill (tons)---- 1,900-2,200; Americus mill (tons)---- 1,200-1,400; Pocahontas mill (tons)---- 600- 700; 3,700-4,300	78 at $3.50 to $7.25.	Underground crushing, 3 Traylor Bulldog crushers, 36 by 48 inch openings, to crush to 3½-inch size; 4 6B Allis-Chalmers gyratory, crush to 3 inch; 2 6B Allis-Chalmers gyratory, crush to 2½ inch.	South mill, 120 stamps; Americus mill, 240 stamps; Pocahontas mill, 160 stamps; total 520 stamps, 1,570 pounds each, grind to ⅝ or ⅞ inch mesh; 8 Allis-Chalmers 5 by 10 foot rod mills, 3 Allis-Chalmers 5 by 14 foot tube mills, final product 80 percent minus 100 mesh, 40 percent minus 200 mesh.
5. Alaska-Juneau mine, Juneau, Alaska.	Free gold in gash and fissure veins in black slate and brown metagabbro. Some gold very coarse. Metagabbro hard to crush.	Small cut from concentrators, barrel amalgamated to recover 61 percent of gold, which is free. Concentrates shipped to smelter.	13,000 tons handled, of which 57 percent is hand sorted, leaving milling necessity of 6,000 tons.	9 foremen, 75 men.	3 type C Buchanan jaw-crushers, 36 by 48 inch, set to 8 inch; 9 K Gates type gyratory, set to 2 inch.	Two 4-foot Symons cone crushers set to 1 inch; two 24 by 60 inch Traylor AA Ajax type, set to make 50 to 30 percent minus 100 mesh; eleven 8 by 6 foot ball mills, to grind to 7 mesh; five 6 by 12 foot ball mills, to grind to 7 mesh; 2 Allis-Chalmers 5 by 5 foot ball mills.

6. Lucky Shot mine, Willow Creek district, Alaska. — Quartz veins in quartz diorite. Free gold with 1½ percent rich sulphide. — Amalgamation 85 percent, from first cut, and +5 percent by cyanidation. — 35 tons — 1 superintendent, 6 men. — 9 by 16 inch jawcrusher. — No. 53 Marcy ball mill.

Type and capacity of concentration	Costs per ton of ore milled					Metallurgical data					
	Labor	Power, lights, and water	Supplies	Miscellaneous	Total	Head value by assay	Mill extraction (percent)	Tailings loss per ton	Bullion recovered per ton of ore	Reagent consumed per ton of ore (troy pounds)	Iron consumed per ton of ore treated (pounds)
1. 36 Frue vanners for slimes; Wilfley table for sands	$0.23	$0.19	$0.10	$0.44	$0.96	$6.26	89.03	$0.68	$3.82	Hg----a 0.113	0.704
2.	.26	.37	.57	.19	1.39	11.38	89.27	1.22	10.16	Cyanide 1.345 / Lime 5.987 / Zn .070 / PbNO₃ .009	.496
3.					.939	6.00	96.35		----	Cyanide .500 / Zn .025 / PbNO₃ .003	1.8
4.	.272	.071	.227	.011	.581	4.90	93	.34	b 2.62	Cyanide .3885 / Lime 2.74 / Zn .0303 / Hg --c .078	c .323 / d .364
5. 88 Deister Simplex sand tables; 13 Deister reconcentrate tables handle high-grade concentrates; 2 Deister slime tables; 2-cell Mineral Separation Sub A flotation machine.	.108	.029	.099		.236	1.10	78.51	.24	.86		
6. Gibson table; 4-cell Mineral Separation Sub A flotation machine.						25.00 / 200.00 e	97	.90			

a Ounces.   b By amalgamation and cyanidation.   c By amalgamation and cyanidation.   d Tube mill.   e Stamps.

1. U.S. Bur. Mines Inf. Circ. 6476, July 1931.
2. U.S. Bur. Mines Inf. Circ. 6508, September 1931.
3. U.S. Bur. Mines Inf. Circ. 6541, October 1931.
4. U.S. Bur. Mines Inf. Circ. 6408, February 1931.
5. U.S. Bur. Mines Inf. Circ. 6236, February 1930.
6. Unpublished data from I. C. Ray, U.S. Geol. Survey.

The adequate planning and design of the mills in the Fairbanks district have, up to the present time, received only scant attention. The ores mined in the past were of high grade, and tailing losses of 15 percent, more or less, were not considered of much importance. So far as is known to the writer, no mill in the district is operating any device for saving concentrates, though the primary ore carries as much as 2 percent of sulphides, some of which are rich in gold. Naturally there are large tailing losses. Sampling of some of the mill tailing dumps indicates that they will in all probability be reworked when those properties are put on an effective operating basis.

The mills that were in operation in the Fairbanks district in 1931 were the Ready Bullion and Mohawk, on Ester Dome, and the Cleary Hill, Soo, and Crites & Feldman, in the Pedro Dome area. The equipment of these mills is shown in the following table, together with that of some of the nonoperating mills.

Gold quartz mills in the Fairbanks district, Alaska, in 1931

Ester Dome region

Name of mill	Coarse crushing	Fine grinding	Gold-saving equipment	Power plant	Capacity
Ready Bullion	Jawcrusher	2 Nissen stamps, 20 mesh.	12 by 4 foot plate.	Wood, steam, 30 horsepower.	15 tons, 10-hour shift.
Mohawk	do	8-foot Lane Chile type mill, 20 mesh.	do	Semi-Diesel, 15 horsepower.	20–30 tons 24 hours.
St. Paul	do	do	do	Wood, steam, 20 horsepower.	10 tons, 10-hour shift.
Elmes	do	5 stamps	do	Wood, steam, 30 horsepower.	15–20 tons 24 hours.

Pedro Dome region

Name of mill	Coarse crushing	Fine grinding	Gold-saving equipment	Power plant	Capacity
Soo	Jawcrusher	2 stamps, 20 mesh.	8 by 3-foot plate.	Gasoline, 10 horsepower.	5–10 tons, 24 hours.
Cleary Hill	7 by 9 inch Blake jawcrusher.	5 stamps, 20 mesh.	12 by 4-foot plate.	Diesel, 100 horsepower.	15–20 tons, 24 hours.
Crites & Feldman (old).	do	do	do	Coal, steam, 30 horsepower.	Do.
Crites & Feldman (new).	do	Gibson rod mill, 30 mesh.	12 by 3-foot plate.	Gasoline, 15 horsepower.	5–10 tons, 20-hour shift.
Newsboy	7 by 9-inch Dodge jawcrusher.	5 stamps, 20 mesh.	12 by 4-foot plate.	Wood, steam, 40 horsepower.	15–20 tons 24 hours.
Gibson	do	do	do	Wood, steam, 30 horsepower.	Do.
Chatham (dismantled).	7 by 9-inch Blake jawcrusher.	10 stamps			
Wyoming	Jawcrusher	Herman pebble mill.	8 by 2-foot plate.	Gasoline, 10 horsepower.	5–10 tons, 24 hours.
Tolovana	6 by 7-inch jawcrusher.	2 Nissen stamps.	10 by 4-foot plate.	Wood, steam, 40 horsepower.	15 tons, 24 hours.

None of these mills have any concentrating devices, and in most of the mills no provision was made for even storing tailings.

As nearly as could be learned from the meager records kept at the mills the best savings are about 85 percent, and it is estimated that at some plants losses ran as much as 25 percent of the head values.

From available data of mill practice on ores of similar character it would seem that the greatest savings at lowest costs can be obtained by removing the coarse free gold as quickly as possible after primary coarse crushing to about 20 mesh. This should be followed by rough concentration, either on tables or by flotation methods, to remove as much gangue mineral as possible, followed by regrinding, amalgamation, and probably cyanidation of the fine concentrates.

Owing to the extremely cold weather in winter in the Fairbanks district it is difficult to maintain an adequate water supply at a reasonable cost. It is suggested that with deeper mining, when pumping will be necessary, it may be possible to store mine water underground and possibly to install mill equipment underground, where temperatures can be controlled more economically than on the surface.

GOLD LODE DEPOSITS

GENERAL CHARACTER

The gold lodes of the Fairbanks district are fissure veins or lodes, cutting various types of schists of pre-Cambrian age, usually in fairly close proximity to bodies of intrusive acidic igneous rock. The narrower veins, from 2 inches to 3 feet wide, are by far the most productive source of lode gold so far developed. In a few mines, notably the Billy Sunday, Newsboy, and Hi-Yu, silicified schist in which there are closely spaced quartz veinlets, constituting "lodes" in the strict sense, has been found sufficiently rich to mine over widths of 8 to 12 feet. There are several broad zones of silicified, sericitized schist which have been considered as possible gold lodes. Some of these, such as the Ryan Lode, are badly crushed and faulted. In the Ryan Lode the zone is 40 to 70 feet wide, in the Zimmerman cut 60 feet wide, and at the Faulkner property 75 feet wide. Under very favorable mining conditions some of these broad zones might be mined, but under present conditions in the Fairbanks district it seems very doubtful whether even the richest, the Ryan Lode, could be worked at a profit.

DISTRIBUTION

There is strong evidence to show the close relation of structure both to the intrusion of the igneous rocks and to the formation of the veins and lodes in the Fairbanks district. A study of plate 3 will direct attention first to the nearly parallel alinement of the larger intrusive masses and the mineralized zone northeast of Fairbanks along eastward-trending lines. These trends were evidently predetermined by fracturing along or near the crests of low anticlines, which are details of the general structure described by Prindle and Katz. On Ester Dome all the trend lines, both of intrusive bodies and of vein systems, are northward, conforming to what appears to be a cross fold in the major structure of the ridge between the Yukon and Tanana Rivers.

Brooks [14] recognized this structural control and adequately described the general structure of the lode system at some length.

On figures 3 and 4 have been plotted the directions and dips of the principal veins and faults that were examined in the Fairbanks district in 1931. This diagram clearly illustrates the great difference in major trend lines between the Pedro Dome area and the Ester Dome area. In the Pedro Dome area practically all the principal veins strike between N. 60° W. and west and dip south. There are a few veins that strike N. 25° E. to N. 45° E. with westerly dips. The major postmineral faulting in the Pedro Dome area likewise has a west-northwest trend almost parallel to the trend of mineralization, but there are also numerous faults striking in almost every direction.

In Ester Dome the greatest number of veins strike between north and N. 40° E., with dips both east and west. There are, however, some veins that strike northwest, but all of these dip to the northeast. The postmineral faults on Ester Dome are more regular than in the Pedro Dome area, for all those plotted fall between N. 35° W. and N. 50° E.

VEIN FILLING AND DETAILS OF STRUCTURE

The higher-grade gold ores throughout the district are very similar in appearance and mineralization. All of them consist of white quartz showing various degrees of crushing. The ores are stained brownish red with limonite near the surface, and the better-grade rock is everywhere stained a peculiar greenish yellow by oxides of antimony and arsenic. Sulphides, where they are visible, are usually seen to accompany a fine-grained grayish-white quartz in veinlets. Visible free gold is in general closely associated with the sulphides but is occasionally found by itself in the midst of white quartz. The proportion of sulphides in the ore is never more than 2 per cent and usually less than 1 percent. The sulphides are rich and should be saved, particularly as free gold in a fine state of subdivision is included in them.

---

[14] Brooks, A. H., Antimony deposits of Alaska : U.S. Geol. Survey Bull. 649, pp. 20–23, 1916.

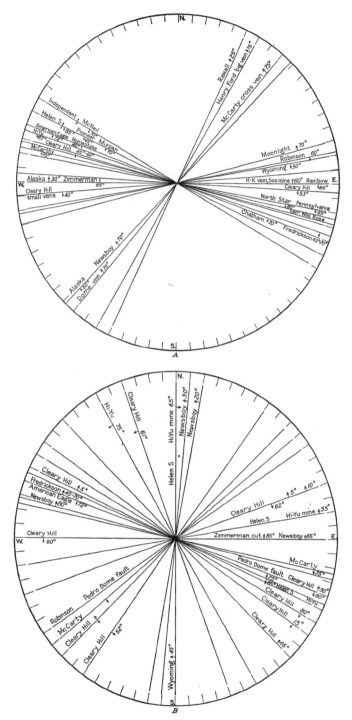

FIGURE 3.—Directions and dips of veins and faults in the Pedro Dome area, Fairbanks district. *A*, veins; *B*, faults.

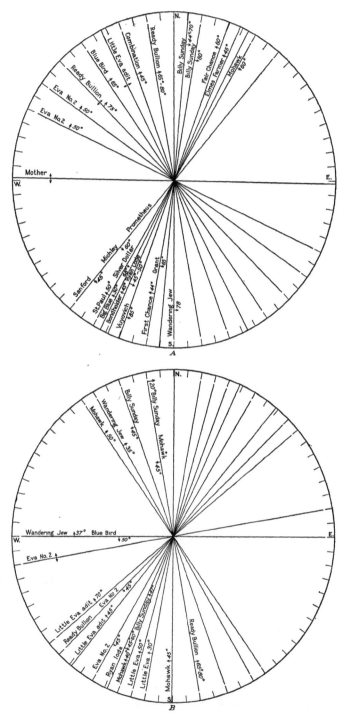

FIGURE 4.—Directions and dips of veins and faults in the Ester Dome area, Fairbanks district. *A*, veins; *B*, faults.

A study of thin sections and polished faces of vein quartz shows conclusively that there have been at least four periods of introduction of silica. The earliest deposit was a rather coarsely crystalline white quartz that does not appear to have been accompanied by metallic minerals. This quartz was later brecciated and crushed by earth movements. The next quartz was deposited in somewhat smaller crystals in the breccia of the earlier quartz with a little pyrite and some free gold. These second veins were again crushed and later healed with still finer grained grayish or white quartz accompanied by the sulphides and free gold which made the bonanza ores of the lodes. Still later there was some reopening of the veins and deposition of small dog-tooth crystals of white quartz in open fractures which were not entirely filled. This quartz apparently represents the last of the mineralizing solutions and does not appear to have carried any metallic minerals.

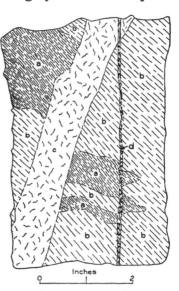

FIGURE 5.—Structural relations of vein quartz in Fairbanks district. Simple veins of two ages cutting across schistosity. a, Dark silicified schist; b, light-colored sericitized schist; c, early white quartz vein with vugs; d, later white quartz vein with many vugs.

Most of the veins cut directly across the schistosity and occupy persistent, relatively straight fracture planes. (See fig. 5.) In places, however, the schist is cut in many directions by stringers of quartz. There are some veins that in general are nearly parallel to the schistosity, but they are rare and usually of small size, both in thickness and in lateral extent. At most places these veins parallel to the schistosity are offshoots from the larger veins that cut the formations and are likely to carry a galena-jamesonite heavy sulphide ore rather than the usual quartz, sulphide, and free gold ore. In detail these veins cut across the planes of schistosity. (See fig. 6, A.)

In most veins there is a rough sheeting due to crushing and recementation by quartz of different character. There may have been an original banded deposition of earlier quartz, as is indicated by fragments of terminated crystals, but such banding has been destroyed by later brecciation, though the barren quartz deposited during the fourth or final stage of mineralization in places has escaped crushing.

The third stage of silica deposition appears to have been of greatest importance in the formation of ore. The mineralizing agent, in addition to silica, carried a considerable burden of iron, arsenic, antimony, and sulphur, together with gold and some lead and bismuth. Apparently this mineralization was not so wide-spread as that of the earlier periods, for it is only in places of more intense brecciation of the two older phases of quartz that the sulphide gold quartz of this third stage is strongly developed. There are many veins of low to medium grade ore, but the relatively few bonanza ore bodies appear to have been formed only where the third stage of mineralization was most intense.

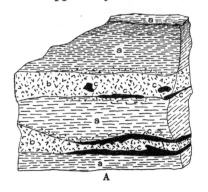

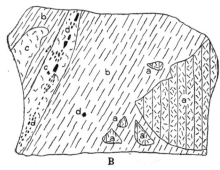

FIGURE 6.—Metallization of veins with sulphides and free gold, Fairbanks district. A, Tolovana mine. a, Gray quartz-mica schist, some sulphides near quartz veins; b, quartz veins; c, mixed sulphides, quartz, and free gold. B, H-K vein, Soo mine. a, Dark-gray silicified schist; b, iron-stained white quartz crushed parallel to direction of vein; c, later white drusy quartz with abundant sulphide and free gold; d, free gold, platy and crystalline.

Typical specimens of the bonanza type of metallization are illustrated in figures 7 and 8. The ore illustrated from the Tolovana mine (fig. 6, A) is unusual because the veinlets are parallel to the schistosity of the enclosing rocks and because intense crushing, except along the contacts between quartz and schist is conspicuous by its absence. It is believed that this specimen represents an offshoot of the third period of metallization, because no quartz having the appearance of that characteristic of the two earlier periods is present.

The ore from the H-K vein of the Soo mine (fig. 6) is more typical of the bonanza ore of the district. It is an iron-stained quartz with much greenish-yellow antimony-arsenic oxide and visible free gold in close association with sulphides along a definite band in the vein. The polished surface shows that the dark schist wall was silicified, brecciated, and cemented by white quartz and a little gold, later iron-stained, and that this vein was again crushed and brecciated in a definite band along which fine-grained quartz with pyrite, arsenopyrite, stibnite, and free gold was deposited.

The free gold in bonanza ore is usually found in close association with the sulphides but occurs also without sulphides. It was in part deposited with the second generation of quartz, but the bulk of it is believed to have come in with the third generation. Both types of occurrence are illustrated in figures 7 and 8.

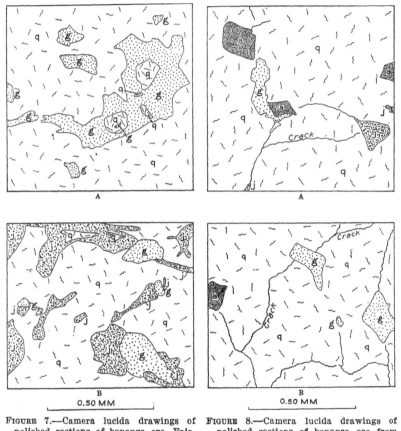

FIGURE 7.—Camera lucida drawings of polished sections of bonanza ore, Fairbanks district. A, H-K vein, Soo mine; B, Billy Sunday mine. g, Gold; j, jamesonite; q, quartz.

FIGURE 8.—Camera lucida drawings of polished sections of bonanza ore from Bank stope, Cleary Hill mine. a, Arsenopyrite; g, gold; j, jamesonite; q, quartz.

The gold in the ores illustrated in figure 7 is clearly primary gold. That from the H-K vein came from a depth of only 30 feet and that from the Billy Sunday mine was obtained below the water level, at 200 feet below the outcrop.

The specimen of bonanza ore illustrated in figure 8 is from the Bank stope on the Penrose level of the Cleary Hill mine, about 150 feet below the surface on the dip of the vein. Although this part of the vein is badly crushed, the polished sections indicate that the sulphides are not oxidized and that the gold and sulphides are primary.

Postmineral movement has been widespread, and almost everywhere the veins are accompanied by clay selvages and gouge on the walls. It is rare to find ore frozen to the wall rock. Postmineral brecciation of the quartz and country rock has permitted ground water to penetrate along certain parts of veins to the greatest depths attained by the mine openings.

Oxidation products, chiefly limonite and the yellowish-green arsenical and antimonial oxides and occasionally manganese oxide, can be seen in the lowest levels of the Cleary Hill, Mohawk, and Hi-Yu mines. However, a relatively small part of the vein filling has been completely oxidized, even in the shallow surface pits on outcrops of the veins.

Unquestionably there has been some mechanical concentration of gold as a result of weathering in surface parts of the veins. There has also been a little concentration of gold by downward-moving surface waters in certain highly brecciated zones along some veins, but such concentration is not believed to have materially affected the great majority of veins in the Fairbanks district. At one place near the mouth of the lower tunnel of the Ready Bullion mine a small amount of secondary gold has been deposited with manganese oxide on joint planes in the schists near the main vein. This is the only place where secondary gold was positively recognized. Some of the very rich ore near the surface of the H-K vein of the Soo mine, which it was thought might contain secondary gold, was found to be rich because of an unusually large amount of primary free gold deposited with sulphides.

An attempt was made, by a study of the records of fineness of gold and silver in bullion, to determine whether or not downward enrichment had been of importance in the best-developed mines. This study did not yield conclusive results, because the records were not complete and in many mines ores from various stopes are mixed before milling, so that exact relation of fineness to locality could not be determined.

The schist wall rocks near the veins have been altered to a surprisingly small extent, except in the broad zones of crushing and silicification such as are found at the Faulkner property, the Zimmerman cut, and the Pedro Dome fault. In these broad zones the schist and intrusive rocks have been sericitized and silicified so as to be hardly recognizable. Along the typical veins, which are from 1 to 3 feet wide, the enclosing rocks have been bleached to some extent by the formation of sericite and a very little calcite and by the introduction of silica, though silicification is not noticeable at all places. Small cubical crystals of pyrite are sparingly disseminated in some of the more highly altered wall rocks.

MINERALS OF THE LODE DEPOSITS

The following is a list of minerals that have been found in the ores of the Fairbanks district. The nature of the work precluded a complete study of the minerals in all the specimens collected.

Argentite (silver glance, Ag_2S).—Possibly present in ore from the Prometheus vein, on Ester Dome, but in such small amount that a definite determination could not be made. The presence of this mineral would account for the high silver content of the Prometheus ore.

Arsenopyrite (mispickel, arsenical pyrite, FeAsS).—One of the most widespread minerals found in the ores of the Fairbanks district but not present in large quantities at any locality. Usually occurs with stibnite and free gold in grayish to white quartz of the third generation, in small veins cementing brecciated earlier quartz. The fine-grained gray quartz is usually not well crystallized, but under the microscope well-developed rhombic forms are occasionally seen, particularly in the richer gold ores.

Bismuth (Bi).—Native bismuth has been found in certain of the placer concentrates on Pearl Creek, tributary of Fish Creek, and on the upper part of Gilmore Creek, about 2 miles west of the Fish Creek locality. The particles are brownish gray, are about the size of a large pinhead, and in the ore seen on Gilmore Creek nearly surrounded a small gold nugget. On Melba Creek native bismuth and bismuthinite (bismuth sulphide) are reported to occur in very rich gold-bearing vein quartz. Specimens of this rock tested in the laboratory of the Geological Survey also showed the presence of considerable tellurium, but its mineral association was not determined.

Boulangerite ($5PbS.2Sb_2S_3$).—A bluish-gray lead-antimony sulphide crystallizing in plumose forms, not easily recognized in hand specimens and not common in the ores from the Fairbanks district which have been studied. Recognized in a polished section of ore from the Ready Bullion mine, mixed with arsenopyrite and stibnite carrying free gold.

Calcite ($CaCO_3$).—An uncommon, inconspicuous gangue mineral, never seen in large masses and rarely visible to the naked eye. Certain ores viewed in thin section under the microscope are seen to contain a little calcite intergrown with quartz. Calcite was also in thin sections of altered quartz-mica schists that were largely converted to fine-grained aggregates of sericite, quartz, chlorite, and calcite.

Cervantite (Sb_2O_4).—A canary-yellow oxidation product surrounding masses of stibnite in layers as much as half an inch thick. Also occurs as the peculiar yellowish-green stain found in all the high-grade ores of the Fairbanks district and one of the favorable signs most looked for by the miners and prospectors in quartz outcrops.

Chalcocite (copper glance, Cu_2S).—This lead-gray copper sulphide is rare in the Fairbanks district, having been found only in ore from the Prometheus vein, on Ester Dome, which carries an unusual amount of silver.

Chalcopyrite (copper pyrites, $Cu_2S.Fe_2S_3$).—Recognized in massive form at the Westonvitch property, on upper Cleary Creek, where it is mixed with pyrite, sphalerite, and galena, but usually not a common constituent of the ores of the Fairbanks district.

Covellite (CuS).—A blue copper sulphide not usually found in the ores of the Fairbanks district but recognized in a polished section of high-grade ore from the Bank stope of the Cleary Hill mine and in ore from the Prometheus vein.

Galena (PbS).—The cubical crystals of galena are found rather sparingly in the ores of this district but occur mixed with jamesonite in certain of the narrow veins that lie parallel to the schistosity on the divide between Cleary Creek and upper Fairbanks Creek.

Gold (Au).—Native gold is wide-spread in the veins of the Fairbanks district. It occurs in association with various sulphides in the primary ores of the district. It was evidently deposited with the sulphides and quartz, principally in the third period of vein reopening and filling, but some native gold also accompanied the second generation of quartz. Like all gold in nature, that from the Fairbanks district contains some silver. Fineness of the bullion from the lodes as reported ranges from 0.780 to 0.906, with the average about 0.810 to 0.820.[15] The fineness of gold varies from one vein to another, and wherever the records are complete and the ore from different veins has been milled separately it is possible to distinguish the vein from which the bullion came by its fineness.

Jamesonite (lead-antimony sulphide, $4PbS.FeS.3Sb_2S_3$).—Fairly common in the Fairbanks district. Much of the finely granular gray sulphide of the third generation of mineralization consists of an intimate mixture of arsenopyrite, jamesonite, and stibnite with free gold. Jamesonite also occurs massive with galena in certain veins and veinlets parallel to the schistosity in the region at the headwater tributaries of Cleary Creek and upper Fairbanks Creek. The mineral is rarely pure but is included in a fine-grained granular gray aggregate.

Limonite (iron hydroxide, $Fe_2O_3.nH_2O$).—Iron stain is prevalent in all the ores of the Fairbanks district from the surface to the deepest workings. Although the red-brown stain is seen everywhere it is not abundant at any place. Limonite was apparently formed chiefly as a decomposition product of pyrite and arsenopyrite. As the iron-bearing sulphides are not abundant in the primary ores, it follows that limonite is not abundant in the oxidation products.

Löllingite ($FeAs_2$).—This iron arsenide resembles arsenopyrite in form and color and cannot be distinguished from that mineral except by microchemical tests. It is apparently present in more or less abundance in all the sulphide ores of the district.

Manganese oxide.—Black manganese stains in brecciated vein material and wall rock are not uncommon in the Fairbanks district. They were noted principally in the heavily brecciated wall rock at the Ready Bullion and Mohawk mines, on Ester Dome. A little manganese oxide was also recognized in some of the brecciated ores in the Cleary Hill mine. In general, however, manganese oxides are rather rare in association with the ores of the district. At the Ready Bullion mine manganese oxide was seen with what was believed to be secondary gold on joint planes in the schist wall rock adjacent to one of the veins. The ores of the district have not been studied sufficiently to identify the various manganese oxides that may be found in ore deposits of this type.

Mariposite.—A green chrome mica occurs sparingly as a gangue mineral in some of the higher-grade ores of the district. It was definitely determined associated with quartz in specimens from the Zimmerman cut, Ryan lode, Stay vein on Little Eva claim, and Flower vein near the St. Paul mill.

Pyrite (iron pyrites, FeS_2).—Found in small quantities in all the ores of the district, both in quartz veins and replacing altered schist wall rocks. It usually occurs as small cubical crystals and only rarely in massive form. At the Westonvitch property, on upper Cleary Creek, however, it occurs in large masses, mixed with sphalerite, galena, and chalcopyrite.

---

[15] Smith, P. S., Fineness of gold in the Fairbanks district, Alaska: Econ. Geology, vol. 8, p. 450, 1913.

Quartz (SiO₂).—Quartz is the most common gangue mineral of the ores of the Fairbanks district. It has replaced schists and igneous rocks in close proximity to the veins, but in general such replacement is not so prevalent as in many mining camps. In the veins proper four generations of quartz have been recognized, each later generation recementing brecciated crushed quartz and wall rock of the preceding generations. The earliest quartz was apparently a coarsely crystalline barren milky-white variety that was probably deposited in drusy form in open veins. Few if any of these druses remain intact, for all the veins have been broken during the subsequent movements and crushing. The second generation of quartz is a little finer grained than the first and does not appear to have been so well crystallized. It carries a little pyrite and some free gold, though as a rule not enough gold to make an ore. The third generation is still finer grained, is grayish white, and carries most of the gold and all the sulphides now found in the veins. It was the ore maker of the district. The fourth generation of quartz was evidently produced as the end product of the period of mineralization. It occurs as crystals in narrow open veinlets cutting all the other varieties of quartz and sulphides. It does not carry ore minerals.

Scorodite (FeAs₂O₈).—Leek-green to white arsenic oxide stains are common in all the gold-quartz ores of the district, but they cannot be distinguished readily from the antimony oxides on casual inspection. Under the microscope and by blowpipe tests the mineral was identified in ores taken from nearly every mine. It is not an abundant or commercially important mineral but is one of the constituents of the richer ores of the district.

Sphalerite (ZnS).—Small quantities of sphalerite in dark-colored crystals of typical tetrahedral form are not an unusual constituent of much of the sulphide ore in the district. Definite crystals of zinc sulphide are rarely recognized in the ores without the aid of a microscope. At the Westonvitch property, on upper Cleary Creek, a considerable amount of well-crystallized black massive sphalerite occurs more or less mixed with pyrite, chalcopyrite, and galena.

Stibiconite (H₂Sb₂O₅).—This mineral occurs in association with cervantite and usually cannot be distinguished from it except by chemical means.

Stibnite (Sb₂S₃).—A lead-gray mineral commonly in bladed crystals, of widespread occurrence in the gold ores of the Fairbanks district. Also found at many places in the veins in segregated masses of the nearly pure mineral. These lenticular bodies have been the source of much of the antimony ore shipped from the district. Certain veins, notably at the Eagle (Scrafford) antimony mine on Eagle Creek, the McQueen and St. Paul veins on Ester Dome, the Frederickson mine, near Dome, and several veins at the head of Cleary and Fairbanks Creeks, have contained large lenses of nearly pure stibnite.

Teetrahedrite (gray copper ore, 5Cu₂S.2(Cu,Fe,Zn)S.2Sb₂S₃).—A very rare constituent of some veins rich in silver. Identified only in ore from the Prometheus vein, on Ester Dome, in very sparing amounts with chalcocite and the more common sulphides.

SAMPLING

The primary object of this investigation was to determine the extent of ore at various mines in the Fairbanks district and to obtain some estimate of the ore tonnage that the district as a whole might yield. It was of course realized that ore is not the only tonnage of significance to the Alaska Railroad, for obviously the operation of several mines employing a number of men each would mean a considerable increase in inbound freight.

It was early recognized that it would be impracticable in this work to sample each property in as thorough a manner as a private engineer would use on an examination for purchase. Sufficient samples were cut from veins to give a general idea of their tenor and as a check on statements from other sources as to the value. Special sampling was done on some of the wide lodes which it was thought might show ore bodies of sufficient size and tenor to warrant investigation with a view to large-scale mining operations.

Calculations of tonnage where given in this report are correct so far as the data available warrant, but the values as stated are based on incomplete evidence and must be subject to revision through closer spacing of samples. At best the sampling of veins carrying free gold is difficult, and for accurate determination of average value of ore close spacing of samples on the veins is essential. With the most careful sampling attainable of deposits of this type, it is rarely possible to get more than approximately identical results even when resampling the same cuts. For the purpose of arriving at the most trustworthy estimate of the value of the ores, it is believed better to accept averages of mill recovery and stope tonnage than to depend on the assays of small samples.

MINES AND PROSPECTS

During the present study the writer visited all the lode mines and prospects of the district of whose existence he could learn and studied the surface exposures and the underground workings insofar as they were accessible. Plate 3 shows the location of all the active mines and of the more important prospects. Maps of the various groups of claims in the Pedro Dome area are printed herewith, insofar as they could be obtained, and figure 18 shows the location of the mines and prospects in the Ester Dome area. Below is a list of the lode claims of the Fairbanks district in 1931, with such information as to their ownership as could be collected.

Lode claims in Fairbanks district, 1931

[P, producing; D, developing; X, prospecting]

Pedro Dome area

	Name	Ownership as reported
X	North Star Extension	H. F. Faulkner.
X	North Star	Do.
X	David	Northern Commercial Co. one half, Robinson and Drouin one half.
	Rainbow	Jack Nirige and Hershberger.
	La Rose	Reliance Mining Co. (Spaulding mine), patented mineral survey 816 (represented by M. E. Stevens).
P	Wild Rose	Do.
P	Soo	Do.
	Waterbury	Do.
	Carnation	Do.
	Waverly	Do.
	Equity Association Placer	Do.
D	Omega	M. E. Stevens.
D	Alpha	Do.

Lode claims in Fairbanks district, 1931—Continued

Pedro Dome area—Continued

	Name	Ownership as reported
	Dorando	Crites & Feldman.
	Sunnyside	Do.
D	Summit	Do.
	Nars	Do.
P	Hi-Yu	Do.
	Insurgent	Do.
P	Teddy R	Do.
P	Helen S	Do.
	Yankle Doodle Fraction	Do.
	Chatham No. 2	Chatham Mining Co., patented mineral survey 1713, Mrs. Burns.
	Fey	Do.
	Colby No. 2	Do.
	Fay No. 2	Do.
	Colby	Do.
	Wolf	A. J. Nordale estate, patented mineral survey 1607.
	Keystone	Do.
	Kawilita	Do.
	Fairbanks	Do.
	Hope	Do.
P	Free Gold	Cleary Hill Mining Co., patented mineral survey 821.
	Snow Drift	Cleary Hill Mining Co.
	Colorado	Do.
D	Wyoming	Cleary Hill Mining Co., one half; Wackwitz Bros., one half.
	Wyoming Fraction	Cleary Hill Mining Co.
	New York	Do.
	Free Gold Fraction	Do.
P	Texas	Do.
	California	Do.
	Paupers Dream	Do.
	Alabama	Do.
	Idaho	Do.
	Henry Ford No. 4	F. J. McCarty.
P	Golden Eagle	Do.
D	Henry Ford No. 3	Do.
D	Henry Ford No. 1	Do.
	Henry Ford	Do.
	Henry Ford No. 2	Do.
	Caribou No. 1	Do.
	Caribou No. 2	Do.
	Marigold	Do.
D	Pioneer	Do.
	Pennsylvania	Do.
	Willie	Do.
	Henry Clay	Do.
	Free Gold	Do.
	Laughing Water	Do.
	Minnie Ha Ha	Do.
	Mazeppa (old Bill Toft)	Unknown.
	Blue Moon	Do.
	Trojan No. 1	Do.
	Trojan	Do.
	Empire (old New York)	Do.
	Empire No. 1 (old North Star)	Do.
	I.X.L. (old Union)	Do.
	Grismoe	Do.
D	Alaska (old Jupiter-Goldstone)	Wackwitz.
D	Alaska No. 2 (old Goldstone)	Do.
D	Alaska No. 3 (old Mars-Emerald)	Do.
	Tolovana 1	Tolovana Mining & Milling Co., Martin Pinska.
	Tolovana 2	Do.
	Tolovana 3	Do.
	Tolovana 4	Do.
P	Scheuyemeress 1	Do.
	Scheuyemeress 2	Do.
	Scheuyemeress 3	Do.
	Scheuyemeress 4	Do.
P	Scheuyemere 1	Do.
	Scheuyemere 2	Do.
	Scheuyemere 3	Do.
	Scheuyemere 4	Do.
	Westonvitch	Tolovana.
	Oro Grande	Unknown.
	Bob	Do.
	Oro Fino	Do.
	Jack	Do.
D	Lucky Lad (Newsboy)	Newsboy Mining Co., leased to Earl R. Pilgrim.
	Newsboy Extension	Do.
D	Dome View	F. M. Wackwitz.
D	Dome View No. 1	Do.
	Rock Run	Do.
	Rock Run No. 1	Do.

Lode claims in Fairbanks district, 1931—Continued

Ester Dome area

	Name	Ownership as reported
X	Mother Group	Stipp, Logan, and Murphy.
	Grant (B S.)	O. M. Grant.
X	Michley	—— Michley.
P	Sanford	J. H. Sanford.
	Independence	Unknown.
P	Bondholder	Henderson & McGinn, patented mineral survey 1922 (Mohawk Mining Co.).
	Bondholder Extension	Do.
	Peg Leg	Do.
	Yellow Jacket	Do.
	Mohawk No. 3	Do.
	Liberty	Do.
P	Mohawk	Do.
	Mohawk No. 2	Do.
	Spite Fraction	Do.
	George Washington	Unknown.
	St. Paul	John McCann, Thomas, et al.
	Crows Nest	Do.
	Star Light	Do.
	Bald Eagle	Do.
	Blue Lead	Frank Hagel.
	Gold Standard	Do.
	Jolly Roger	McDonald et al., Berry Co.
	Prometheus	Joe McDonald et al.
	Crusaders	Joe McDonald.
	Crusaders Extension	Joe McDonald et al.
X	Clipper	Joe McDonald.
X	Wandering Jew	Do.
	Eclipse	Do.
	Killarney	Do.
X	First Chance	Sam Stay et al., Berry.
	Stibnite Fraction	Unknown.
	Gold Eagle	E. M. Smith et al., patented mineral survey 829.
	Billy Sunday	E. M. Smith et al., patented mineral survey 844.
	Fairview Fraction	E. M. Smith et al.
	Blue Bird Extension	Unknown.
	Hagel Fraction	Do.
	Gem	Ryan Lode Association, patented mineral survey 1602.
	Blue Bird	Jack O'Conner and Mrs. Miller.
P	Fair Chance	McGlone estate (E. M. Smith).
	Ijim	Ryan Lode Association, patented mineral survey 826.
	Eva	Do.
	Edna	Do.
	Star Crystal	Unknown.
P	Blue Bird	John H. McDonald and Lewis Morton (leased to J. Y. Bigelow).
	Rose	Sam Stay.
	Mamie	J Y. Bigelow.
	Monte	Ryan Lode Association, patented mineral survey 826.
	Ryan No. 1	Do.
P	Little Eva	Sam Stay.
	Eva No. 2	Do.
	Blue Bird Extension	John McDonald and Lewis Morton.
D	Comet	Sam Stay.
X	Curlew Granite	Do.
	Curlew No. 2	Do.
	Ryan No. 2	Ryan Lode Association, patented mineral survey 1603.
	Excelsior	Do.
	Merwin	Do.
	St. Patrick	Do.
X	Combination	John H. McDonald and Lewis Morton.
X	McDonald	Do.
	Borovich	?.
	California	?.
	?	Stevens & Borovich.
	Stibnite No. 1	Do.
	Hudson	Do.
	Stibnite No. 2	Do.
	Lode Fraction	Do.
	Ready Bullion	Do.
	Fraction	Do.
	Hosanna	Do.
	Horseshoe	Do.
	Sunflower	Do.
	Mary Stay Fraction	Do.
	Geneva	Do.
	Borovich Fraction	Do.
	North Pole	Do.
	Borovich Lode	Do.
	Borovich No. 2	Do.
	Native Daughter	Do.
	South Pole	Do.
	Camp Claim	Do.

PEDRO DOME AREA

DOME CREEK AND VICINITY

The only lode mine in operation in 1931 in the western part of the Pedro Dome area was the Soo mine, at the head of Dome Creek. (See fig. 9.) Much of the lower portion of this basin is underlain with muck and is covered by large tailings piles from the former placer operations. The quartz diorite mass of Pedro Dome extends along the southern ridge westward nearly to Moose Creek (see pl. 3) and is continued westward by two dikelike masses of quartz porphyry.

SOO

The group of claims locally known as the Soo or Spaulding mine, near the head of Dome Creek, about 1½ miles west-northwest of Pedro Dome, is owned by the Reliance Mining Co. (See fig. 9.)

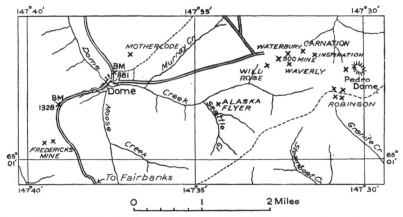

FIGURE 9.—Map of Dome Creek drainage basin, showing location of mines and prospects described in this report.

It is reached by automobile road from Fairbanks by way of Fox, Fox Creek, and Dome, a total distance of approximately 18 miles. The affairs of the Reliance Mining Co. seem to be managed by M. E. Stevens and S. A. Martin so far as relates to most of the claims. The Soo claim, however, is closely controlled by persons in Seattle, Wash., and this divided responsibility has caused some embarrassment. The claims, which have been patented under mineral survey 816, dated June 1913, are the La Rose, Wild Rose, Soo, Waterbury, Carnation, and Waverly lodes and the Equity Association placer. Mr. Stevens also has two claims, the Alpha and Omega, lying south of the west end of the patented group, and these will be included in describing this group of claims. The original owners did some work on the Wild Rose, but most of the development work on the group is said to have been done by lessees. This will account in part for the placing and condition of the workings.

The output from this property was between $75,000 and $100,000 in the period 1912 to 1914 and about $65,000 since 1925. There is a lightweight 3-stamp prospect mill on the property with a 5 by 7 inch crusher and 3 by 8 foot plate, all run by a 10-horsepower gasoline motor. C. M. Hawkins, who had a lease on the H and K vein of the Soo claim in 1931, had also a gasoline-driven hoist, good for about 200 feet of sinking. All the machinery was housed in an old building near the H and K shaft. (See fig. 10.)

This mine was in active operation in 1912, when it was examined by Smith.[16] His description and that of Chapin[17] in 1913 cover many details not now observable on the property.

The only work under way at the Soo mine in the middle of July 1931 was in some shallow shafts on the H and K vein. The terms of Mr. Hawkins' lease were such that only shallow, inexpensive work was justified. Stevens and Martin were also doing a little work on the H and K vein and the Spaulding vein as exposed in the H and K tunnel. (See fig. 10.)

The Hawkins lease covered a short part of the H and K vein west of the tunnel and to a depth of 100 feet. It was impossible to use the old H and K shaft because of the condition of the timbers, so it was used as a water reservoir for the mill, the water being pumped by a small Cornish rig operated by a gasoline engine. The main working at the time of visit on this lease was a new inclined shaft about 150 feet east of the mill, then 30 feet deep. A sample cut by the writer across 14 inches of the crushed iron-stained quartz just above the footwall, as exposed in the bottom of the shaft, assayed $106.76 to the ton. The hanging wall was not exposed in the workings. In late August Mr. Hawkins is reported to have sunk a second shallow shaft about 75 feet west of the old H and K shaft to reach a pillar of ore left by the original Heath and Kerns lease, above a shallow tunnel he had previously run. Just west of the mouth of the tunnel the H and K vein is apparently faulted. What appears to be the same vein was opened on the Omega claim, about 500 feet farther west and 150 feet south of the projection of the H and K vein. It is stated that the H and K shaft is 136 feet deep, with a drift to the east about 400 feet long at the 100-foot level. One ore shoot yielded 400 tons of $36 ore.

In the crosscut tunnel, which cuts the H and K vein about 75 feet below the outcrop, the old drifts are caved, but Stevens and Martin were driving a new drift eastward on the vein. At the face of this

[16] Smith, P. S., op. cit. (Bull. 525), pp. 190–194.
[17] Chapin, Theodore, op. cit. (Bull. 592), pp. 343–345.

40-foot drift the fracture zone strikes east and dips 60° N., cutting quartz-mica schists which have a very low north dip and east strike.

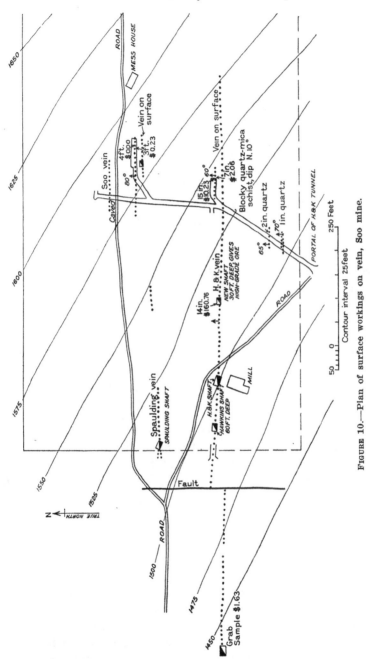

FIGURE 10.—Plan of surface workings on vein, Soo mine.

It consists of 6 to 8 inches of crushed quartz above a well-marked footwall. A sample of this quartz assayed $2.06 to the ton. Above this is 14 to 16 inches of hard, apparently uncrushed white quartz, a sample of which carried only 23 cents to the ton.

The main shaft on the Spaulding or Wild Rose vein was full of water in July 1931 and most of the shallow shafts and surface pits were so badly caved that the vein could not be seen. The vein as exposed in the crosscut tunnel is a fault zone of brecciated schist and quartz about 14 feet in width. The east drift on this vein was about 100 feet long, and in the face there was 7 feet of intensely crushed mica schist with almost no quartz. The zone strikes N. 76° W. and dips 80° N. The upper 4 feet was black, crushed mica schist, which assay showed to be of no value. The lower 3 feet was iron-stained and here and there contained patches of crushed quartz. A sample across this material assayed 23 cents to the ton. It was stated that just east of the tunnel a small block of 28 tons of ore taken out above the drift yielded $80 in the mill. This vein has been traced from the Spaulding shaft eastward on the surface for about 700 feet by open cuts and pits.

The crosscut tunnel continues on to the Soo vein, about 75 feet north of the Spaulding; but the vein could not be examined because of the caved condition of the workings. It is said that the Spaulding shaft is about 200 feet deep and that the ore body has yielded between $70,000 and $80,000.

The high-grade ore being extracted from the ground covered by the Hawkins lease is all much oxidized, yet a study of polished surfaces of specimens of ore very rich in free gold indicates that almost none of the gold is secondary. It is evident from the specimen studied that the primary gold deposition accompanied the arseno-pyrite-stibnite period of metallization, which was one of the last phases of mineralization of this vein. At least 2 and probably 3 periods of deposition of quartz are shown, each followed by brecciation of the older quartz and recementation by younger quartz.

There is practically no ore blocked out, so far as development shows in the Soo mine. Nevertheless the geologic conditions are such that it would appear that properly directed and financed mining is well warranted at this property.

FREDERICKS

The Fredericks mine, on the west side of the ridge between Vault and Dome Creeks (see fig. 9), was idle in the summer of 1931, and from the growth of brush on the dumps appears to have been un-worked for some years. The two shafts and a lower tunnel are all above the ditch of the Fairbanks Exploration Co., on both sides of the now abandoned right of way of the Tanana Valley Railroad near the former Ridge Top station.

All equipment had been removed from the property, and none of the workings were accessible. The dumps are composed entirely of much-weathered quartzite schist considerably stained with iron oxide. At the lower tunnel and shaft, just above the ditch line, there is what appears to be a dump of mill ore totaling about 100 tons. This material is iron-stained schist with quartz carrying arsenopyrite and pyrite, and some of the material has the yellowish-green scorodite stain usually indicative of ore in the district. Two grab samples taken from this dump assayed $1.46 and $2.83 to the ton.

As the mine could not be examined in detail Smith's report of 1912 gives the latest and most complete information available concerning it.[18] He states that the property was developed by 2 shafts, 1 shaft 300 feet deep, with drifts on three levels, and another 100 feet deep. The country rock is a hard quartzitic rock cut by a 7-foot granitic dike. The ground is faulted and slickensided, and the dike is thoroughly decomposed. The vein, in places 3½ feet wide, has a faulted and slickensided zone along its hanging wall, and apparently much of the material removed in mining represented only a shattered zone in the country rock. The zone contains some stibnite, which is apparently more abundant toward the footwall than toward the hanging wall.

So far as is known, no work has been done on this property since 1912.

ROBINSON

Just southwest of the summit of Pedro Dome in the saddle at the head of Granite Creek (see fig. 9) there are a large number of surface pits on a group of claims located by F. C. Robinson in 1930. This ground is said to have been held formerly by a Mr. Nickaloff, who did part of the prospecting. Nearly 100 shallow cuts and several long trenches over an area 1,000 feet long and 300 feet wide expose a fault breccia of highly altered quartz diorite that strikes N. 55° E. There is evidence of some mineralization in this zone, though there is nowhere a large amount of quartz visible. The material on the dumps is for the most part a rusty, sericitized, and in places silicified highly altered igneous rock. Prindle and Katz[19] mapped similar material on the west side of Pedro Dome as altered dike rocks, which they describe as a whitish friable rock, in some places resembling fragments of unslaked lime. Much of it is stained yellowish or reddish by ferruginous matter and contains areas of minutely granular quartz embedded in clear colorless quartz. This

---

[18] Smith, P. S., Lode mining near Fairbanks: U.S. Geol. Survey Bull. 525, pp. 194–196, 1913.

[19] Prindle, L. M., and Katz, F. J., Geology of the Fairbanks district: U.S. Geol. Survey Bull. 525, pl. 1 and p. 73, 1913.

fault breccia appears to mark the same zone as that shown on the west fork of Skoogy Gulch, in the Central Star tunnel, on the southeast side of Pedro Dome, and in the bottom of Skoogy Gulch at the Faulkner property, described on pages 116–117.

In 1931 the main shaft on this property was full of water, the milling equipment had been removed, and all that remained of the mine equipment was a 15-horsepower steam boiler and a hoist.

The ground now held as the Robinson claims apparently includes the lode described by Chapin [20] as the Rose, and by Mertie [21] as the Mohawk. Chapin mentions a shaft 75 feet deep on a vein of quartz that ranged from 4 to 8 feet in thickness and carried considerable free gold. Mertie reports 2 or 3 separate veins on this property and states that 46 tons of ore was mined and milled in 1916.

Chapin also describes briefly several claims in the Little Eldorado Creek drainage basin, including the Sunrise, Thompson, and Hidden Treasure claims.

According to Mr. Nickaloff some very rich float had been found on the ridge now covered by the Robinson claims, but no ore body of workable value had been disclosed in any of the extensive surface prospecting. A sample of what appeared to be the more highly mineralized material picked by the writer as a grab sample from several dumps showed no value upon assay.

About a quarter of a mile north of the summit, on the west side of Pedro Dome, at an elevation of 2,100 feet, there is a short tunnel on altered fault breccia material in a zone that strikes N. 70° W. and dips 75° S. The zone is at least 25 feet wide. A sample of this material, which did not appear highly mineralized anywhere, carried 23 cents to the ton.

Two shafts, both of which were iced up, connected by an open cut or caved stope, were noted about an eighth of a mile north of the Robinson shaft and about half a mile south-southwest of the Newsboy shaft, in the bottom of Last Chance Gulch at an elevation of 2,000 feet. This may be the Sunrise claim mentioned by Chapin.

The tunnel at the main forks of Last Chance Creek mentioned by Chapin as the Hidden Treasure was caved at the mouth and the dump entirely overgrown. It was not visited.

Word was received in September 1931 that some surface prospecting on the ridge between Louise Creek and the West Fork of Last Chance Creek, about a mile east-northeast of the Soo mine, had disclosed a promising vein.

[20] Chapin, Theodore, op. cit. (Bull. 592), p. 342.
[21] Mertie, J. B., Jr., op. cit. (Bull. 662), p. 407.

LITTLE ELDORADO CREEK

OHIO

The Ohio claim is on the ridge at the head of Whisky Gulch between Louis and Spruce Creeks, tributaries of Little Eldorado Creek, about 2 miles northwest of the Soo mine and 3 miles northeast of the old Dome town site. The claims were located by John Rogash in 1916, and an amended location was made May 28, 1927. There are three shallow shafts on a vein that strikes about east. None of the work was accessible, so the dip was not determined, but apparently it is to the south. The ore seen on the dump is an iron and manganese stained quartz, badly crushed and carrying some stibnite and arsenopyrite. A grab sample from about 4 tons of ore in two piles assayed $4.18 a ton.

DOME VIEW

The Dome View and Rock Run group of four claims lies in the head of the west fork of Last Chance Creek, a tributary of Little Eldorado Creek, and is about 1 mile north of Pedro Dome. The claims are held by the Wackwitz Bros., of Cleary post office, who also have the Wyoming mine, on Bedrock Creek. This region has been prospected for some years, and several locations made in the early days were abandoned, as the slide rock, frozen condition of the ground, and steep slopes make prospecting difficult and expensive. Placer gold, found in the gulches on the north side of Pedro Dome, was coarse and angular, and some very rich float has been found at times. These facts kept the Wackwitz Bros. interested, and they finally discovered and located the Dome View vein in 1917. The principal opening is a tunnel at an elevation of 2,000 feet in a steep gulch under the eastern peak of Pedro Dome. A series of open cuts show that the vein continues eastward into the head of the main fork of Last Chance Creek below the Robinson (Rose) shaft on the Last Chance-Skoogy divide.

The Dome View vein strikes N. 40° E. and dips 70° NW., cutting quartz-mica schists that dip 15°–20° S. and strike N. 60° E. The contact of schist and the quartz diorite body that forms the summit of Pedro Dome is only a short distance south of the vein, though its exact position is uncertain because of the heavy talus cover.

The tunnel is 145 feet long and attains a depth of nearly 100 feet. It follows the vein eastward and shows it to range from 12 to 40 inches in width and to average about 30 inches. The white quartz is intensely brecciated in places and heavily iron-stained, particularly along the hanging wall, but in other places it is solid and massive.

Little timber was placed, and parts of the roof are caving, as there are selvages of gouge on both walls of the vein. Three samples cut in places where the vein was least crushed and was safe to sample ran from 38 cents to $3.26 a ton. These were hardly representative samples, as it was unsafe to cut samples in the more highly brecciated parts of the vein, where the better ore might be expected. As a matter of fact, free gold was visible in specimens picked from two such places in the tunnel and from two of the shallow shafts on the surface a short distance east of the tunnel face. The tunnel has developed about 1,300 tons of ore whose value is uncertain but is probably nearer $5 a ton than the $1.47 which the samples taken in the tunnel would indicate.

There is a tunnel driven westward on the vein in the head of the main fork of Last Chance Creek, but it showed little ore.

CLEARY CREEK

Cleary Creek was one of the richest of the placer creeks in the Fairbanks district, and gold-bearing gravel has been found in all its southern tributaries, many of which have been mined. The belt of lodes that supplied the gold to these placers is not much over a mile in width, extending in a low arc concave to the south from the divide between Cleary and Little Eldorado Creeks on the west to the divide between Wolf and Fairbanks Creeks on the east. (See fig. 11.) Although the principal development has been in this belt, there has been more or less prospecting both north and south of it. North of the belt there is very little evidence that mineralization was intense enough to make workable ore deposits. South of the belt mineralization was likewise weak and the veins are relatively small. The writer believes that there is more evidence to encourage further prospecting south of the belt than north of it. The site of mineralization is apparently the axis of a low anticlinal fold. Whether or not the apparent bending is actually due to a change of direction of the axis of the fold could not be determined from the evidence seen. It seems probable, however, that there is a northward-trending fault on the ridge west of Chatham Creek, between the creek and the trail at the summit of the ridge, along which there has been postmineral movement that has given the belt its arcuate form.

After the first period of lode excitement in 1912 died down much of the ground formerly held by many individual locators was abandoned. New locations have been made on some of the ground, and several consolidations of claims have taken place. The only producing lode mine in the Cleary Creek Valley in 1931 were the Cleary Hill (old Rhoads-Hall) mine and the Tolovana property. Develop-

ment work was under way at the Newsboy, and some prospecting was
being carried on at several scattered localities, as mentioned in the
following pages.

The Newsboy group of claims lies just south of the saddle (altitude
1,752 feet) between Cleary Creek and Last Chance Creek (no. 21,
fig. 11). Milepost 22 on the Fairbanks-Circle road (Steese Highway)

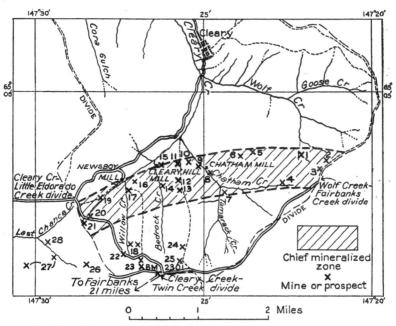

FIGURE 11.—Map of Cleary Creek drainage basin, showing location of mines and prospects
described in this report.

1. Homestake.	10. B.-P.	20. Newsboy Extension.
2. Pennsylvania.	11. California.	21. Newsboy.
3. Doróthy.	12. Pauper's Dream.	22. Cornell.
4. Chatham Mining Co.	13. Alabama.	23. Cheyenne.
5. Alaska.	14. Wyoming.	24. Your Jim.
6. Alaska (old Jupiter-Mars).	15. Cleary Hill.	25. Jackson.
7. Anna-Mary.	16. Tolovana Stibnite.	26. Robinson (Rose).
8. Pioneer.	17. Tolovana.	27. Wackowitz.
9. Reese.	18. Emma.	28. Hidden Treasure.
	19. Westonvitch (Eldorado).	

is on one of the claims. This saddle is 2 miles north-northeast of
Pedro Dome. The Newsboy and Newsboy Extension are the two
principal claims of the group, which comprises a large tract. The
property is owned by the Newsboy Mining Co., but in 1931 it granted
a lease on part to Earl Pilgrim, and he had reopened the Newsboy
shaft to the 160-foot level and was developing the Robinson vein at
the east end of the Newsboy claim.

Mr. Pilgrim had cut through the ice, which filled the shaft to a depth of about 70 feet, and had reopened both the 100-foot (actually 115-foot) level and the 160-foot level. He had not cut out the ice from the old 60-foot level.

The main Newsboy shaft was sunk to a depth of 350 feet early in the mining history of the Fairbanks district and had been equipped with a steam hoist, which was installed in the mill building directly north of the shaft. The mill was later removed to a site on the north side of Cleary Creek opposite the mouth of Willow Creek, about a mile northeast of the mine and 600 feet lower. The old shaft and mill building are now used as a hoist house and blacksmith shop. A rebuilt Buick engine is used to drive a Gardner-Denver air compressor to furnish air to operate a stoper, jackhammer, and the old steam hoist. The old boiler is used as an air receiver. The shaft has a good wooden headframe carrying ore bins and is well timbered to the 160-foot level. Below this level it was under water on June 28 and in the latter part of August 1931, when the writer visited the mine. The ore is hauled to the mill by trucks, which deliver directly to a grizzly over the crusher, which is of a 7 by 9 inch Dodge type. Crushing is done in a 5-stamp Joshua Hendy battery from which the pulp flows over a 5 by 12 foot plate. The deck of a no. 2 Deister table is in the building but appears not to have been in use for some time. A well is located inside the mill building, which also houses a 40-horsepower locomotive-type boiler and pumps. Coal was used for fuel. Mr. Pilgrim had expected to mill some ore during the summer of 1931 but had to leave for other work before repairs on the boiler tubes were completed. A small pile of rather sandy concentrates was found just outside the mill. These were evidently old concentrates, as the pyrite was badly altered and the mass cemented. A grab sample of this pile, which apparently contained about 10 tons, was found by assay to carry $53.98 to the ton. The total production of the Newsboy mine is not known, and many of the old records are said to have been destroyed in a fire. The output of ore must have been fairly large, as the stopes on each side of the shaft are continuous from the surface to the 160-foot level and are reported to go below that level.

As will be seen from figure 12, the vein, which strikes N. 45°–48° E. and dips 65°–80° NW., has been broken by several faults. This vein appears to be near the crest of the anticline, which has determined the site of the Pedro Dome mineralization. The segment of the vein in which the shaft was sunk has been largely stoped, only a few pillars being left to show the character of the ore. The faults northeast of the shaft on both the 100-foot and 160-foot levels have so far proved baffling, for the northeast extension of the vein had not been traced beyond them.   The **main fault** northeast of the shaft strikes west on the 100-foot level **and N. 76° W.** on the 160-foot level and dips 57°–78° N.   It is composed of several planes of movement in a

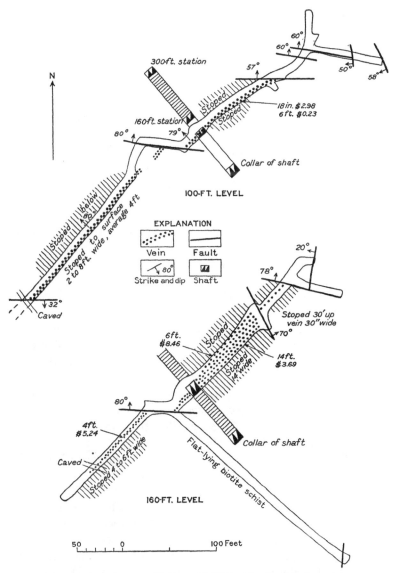

FIGURE 12.—Plan of 100-foot and 160-foot levels, Newsboy mine.

zone 10 feet wide.   In this zone the principal movement, as shown by slickensides, has been horizontal, but many times repeated, with a slightly different direction of dip each time.   Apparently the total resultant of these movements displaced the segment northeast of the fault to the north rather than to the south, although the development work done in attempting to locate it indicates that the owners believed it to be displaced to the south.

Just southwest of the shaft the vein is displaced by a fault striking about N. 60° W. with a dip of 80° N. It consists of 2 inches of gouge on the footwall side, above which there is 10 to 12 inches of crushed schist. This appears to be a reverse fault with a displacement of about 10 feet. At the extreme southwest end of the drift on the 100-foot level there is another east-west fault dipping 32° S. Caving at this point did not permit an examination to determine whether the vein had been picked up beyond the fault or what was the nature of the movement along it. The long crosscut to the southeast on the 160-foot level went through flat-lying, unaltered dark-colored biotite-quartz schist without sign of mineralization.

The Newsboy vein, as exposed on the 160-foot level southwest of the shaft, was 4 to 6 feet wide and consisted of crushed schist and quartz, all more or less iron-stained and containing disseminated pyrite and arsenopyrite. A sample cut across a 4-foot pillar assayed $5.24 to the ton. Northeast of the shaft the vein widened to 12 or 14 feet and consisted of schist with many stringers of quartz parallel to the general strike of the footwall break. The rock was all more or less crushed by postmineral movement. In some places the quartz with arsenopyrite constitutes as much as 60 percent of the lode filling; in other places it constitutes only a small portion of the vein. One sample, cut from a pillar 12 feet below the 160-foot level and 70 feet northeast of the shaft, across 6 feet of ore, mostly quartz, assayed $8.46 to the ton. Another sample taken 100 feet northeast of the shaft across 14 inches on the footwall side of the vein assayed $6.69 to the ton. The stopes above the 160-foot level had been carried two sets wide for some distance above the level. On the 100-foot level the vein for 140 feet northeast of the shaft is from 4 to 6 feet wide and consists of sericitized schist with stringers of quartz, all more or less crushed. The 14 inches next the footwall seemed to be more highly mineralized, as an assay of it showed $2.98 to the ton, whereas a sample cut across the 6 feet of rock being mined assayed only 23 cents a ton. Panning tests of crushed rock and drill cuttings indicate, however, that free gold can be panned from many parts of the 6-foot zone. The stopes to the southwest of the shaft on the 100-foot level were poorly timbered and unsafe. The ore mined ranged from 2 to 8 feet in width and averaged about 4 feet throughout the 200 feet stoped.

The Robinson vein, near the highway about a quarter of a mile east of the Newsboy shaft, has been opened by a shaft about 15 feet deep. It lies about parallel to and north of a small granite porphyry dike (see pl. 3) and strikes N. 79° E. and dips 60° S. It is 10 inches wide, as shown by a 30-foot drift to the west at the bottom of the shaft, and consists of crushed white quartz with some sulphides, in places badly iron-stained. Panning tests indicate that where arsenopyrite is present the ore is of fair grade.

About half a mile east-southeast of the Newsboy shaft and only a short distance south of the granite porphyry dike referred to above there are two quarries beside the Steese Highway, along zones of intense sericitization and silicification of the quartz-mica schists. The northern quarry had been recently worked for road surface material, and a clean face was exposed on June 28, 1931. This showed a zone 32 feet in width, between well-marked slickensided walls, of soft cream-colored sericitized mica schist that is much fractured and contains some quartz veinlets. Both walls of this zone are dark-colored biotite schists that dip north at low angles. It appeared from the bending of the schistosity that there has been reverse faulting along this zone, which strikes N. 80° W. Four samples taken across this face showed no gold or silver upon assay.

Smith [22] has described certain developments at this mine that are not now accessible. His examination included both the 215 and 315 foot levels, now under water. According to his description, the ore there contained large amounts of sulphides, including mainly arseno-pyrite, pyrite, and stibnite, though a little chalcopyrite and sphalerite were recognized.

NEWSBOY EXTENSION

In 1931 the Newsboy Extension mine, about 500 feet northeast of the Newsboy, was not in operation and the workings were inaccessible. Smith,[23] who examined this mine in 1912, states that the vein strikes N. 15° E. and dips 77° W. As this is a different strike from that of the Newsboy vein, he doubts whether it is actually an extension of that vein. Faulting makes it impossible to trace a direct connection between them. It is reported that the shaft on this property is about 115 feet deep, with short drifts both north and south on the 60-foot level. Apparently no work has been done on this property for the last 20 years.

WESTONVITCH

At the forks of Cleary Creek, half a mile east of the Little Eldorado Creek divide, and the same distance west of the junction of Willow and Cleary Creeks, there are three dumps and other indications of former mining at an elevation of about 1,290 feet. These

---

[22] Smith, P. S., op. cit. (Bull. 525), pp. 187–189.
[23] Idem, pp. 189–190.

were on the so-called "Westonvitch property" (one fifth mile north-east of claim 19, fig. 11). The 2 tunnels and 3 shafts could not be entered, and several open cuts were so badly caved that the relation of the ore body to surrounding rocks is uncertain.

The material on the dump is unique, consisting largely of massive pyrite, sphalerite, galena, arsenopyrite, and stibnite that appear to have replaced limestone, which is more or less altered in part to a heavy, black pyroxene-biotite rock. Some bluish crystalline limestone has escaped alteration and replacement, but there is evidence of intense crushing and crumpling of the beds. Several specimens show clearly that there was a period of intense folding on a minute scale after the deposition of the sulphides, and also after the formation of quartz veinlets that cut the sulphides. Gold accompanied the formation of the solid pyrite and pyrite-galena-sphalerite phases but appears to be more abundant in those parts of the ore that are cut by later quartz veinlets, in which arsenopyrite is the principal though sparsely distributed sulphide. Where much sphalerite or galena is present the value in silver increases.

A peculiarity of the massive sulphide ore is that feldspar as well as pyroxene and biotite is always present in it. This locality is not far from the granite porphyry dikes seen on the Steese Highway to the north. It is possible that some of these intrusive rocks are encountered in the underground workings, though no rocks on the dumps could be definitely identified as igneous. The dumps are, however, badly decayed, owing to the large amount of easily weathered sulphides. Most of the rock on the dumps is a heavily iron-stained biotite-quartz schist.

What appears to be this same property was described by Mertie [24] in 1916 under the name Eldorado Mining & Milling Co. At that time a vein from 3 to 12 inches wide was being mined for silver-lead ore but contained also some gold. No record is available of actual shipments of ore from this property.

EMMA

A property at first known as the "Emma claim" and later relocated as the "Katherine claim" lies on the east side of Willow Creek, near the head, at an elevation of 2,100 feet. This property was under development in 1912, when it was examined by Smith.[25] At that time there was a shaft 60 feet deep and about 100 feet of drifts. The east-west vein dips 45°–60° S. and consists of 4 to 12 inches of quartz.

[24] Mertie, J. B., Jr., op. cit. (Bull. 662), p. 416.
[25] Smith, P. S., op. cit., pp. 185–186.

It is reported that 10 tons of selected ore shipped and milled yielded $38 a ton.

This property was reopened in 1924 as the Katherine claim but was soon abandoned, and apparently no work has been done on it since.

CORNELL

A short distance southwest of the Emma claim and west of the road is the Cornell claim, at an elevation of 2,075 feet. A tunnel and several shallow shafts and pits are now caved, and the property has long been abandoned.

TOLOVANA

The camp and main tunnel of the Tolovana Mining Co. are at an elevation of 1,300 feet on Willow Creek, a tributary of Cleary Creek, about 3 miles southwest of Cleary post office and 25 miles by road northeast of Fairbanks (no. 17, fig. 11). The company is represented in Fairbanks by Martin Pinska. The property consists of 13 claims in a compact group 3 claims wide and 4 long, covering approximately 260 acres on upper Cleary Creek and the ridge between Willow and Bedrock Creeks. The claims are the Tolovana 1 to 4, Scheuyemeress 1 to 4, Scheuyemere 1 to 4, and Westonvitch. In 1931 the Tolovana tunnel ground was under lease to Charles W. Nelson and Mr. Parenteau. The mine when in operation by the company produced several thousand dollars, but it had been idle for some years until 1930.

The mill, which is well housed, is equipped with a 6 by 7 inch jaw-crusher, two Nissen stamps of 1,350 pounds each, and two 4 by 10 foot plates. It is operated by a 40-horsepower coal-burning boiler. A well in the mill supplies water during the winter.

The main tunnel runs east on the vein for about 125 feet, then turns north along a fault for about 30 feet, and then eastward on the continuation of the vein for about 350 feet. A shaft near the tunnel mouth was full of water. It is said to be more than 100 feet deep and to connect with a winze sunk at the north-south fault in the tunnel. All of the front part of the tunnel has been iced up, and as the reopening was done with the idea of getting to the face, no unnecessary ice was removed near the mouth. As a consequence, none of the old workings could be inspected, though it was noted that there were stopes below the floor of the tunnel west of the fault. The dark biotite-quartz schist that forms the country rock dips 15° N. The Tolovana vein is in reality a zone of hard schists cut by several stringers of quartz from a quarter to half an inch wide that are subparallel, the zone striking N. 80° E. and dipping 70° S., directly across the schistosity. The veinlets are frozen to the schist, and in places offshoots of quartz lie parallel to the schistosity. The zone of most intense mineralization appears to be about 8 to 12 inches wide and may contain as many as 3 or 4 veinlets in this width, though usually 2 veinlets are persistent. The schist next the veinlets is thoroughly silicified and contains some carbonate, probably calcium carbonate, and minute pyrite crystals disseminated throughout. The veinlets consist of quartz with a little carbonate and arsenopyrite, stibnite, and free gold. The sulphides are most commonly concentrated near the edges of the vein or in the silicified schist next the quartz. The gold occurs free in both the vein quartz and the highly silicified schist between the veinlets.

A tunnel on the west side of Willow Creek, said to be on the Tolovana vein, was caved 75 feet from the mouth, where the vein was first cut about 20 feet below the surface. The ore from this tunnel did not resemble the hard ore from the main Tolovana tunnel.

Smith [26] examined this property in considerable detail in 1912 and visited the workings that are now inaccessible.

JACKSON

At the extreme head of Bedrock Creek, about a quarter of a mile northeast of bench mark 2301 on the divide between Bedrock and Twin Creeks, there are a number of old pits, shafts, and tunnels, all of which were caved and inaccessible in 1931. To judge from the dumps at these workings little had been done at any one of them for several years. One shaft was vertical for 50 feet and then dipped north at a steep angle. The vein strikes N. 70° E., and there is a caved tunnel mouth 100 feet below that was apparently run to crosscut the vein exposed in the shaft. No ore was seen on the dump of the crosscut, and the small amount of ore seen on the dump of the shaft is mostly a mixture of arsenopyrite, jamesonite, and galena. Some prospect pits on gash veins an eighth of a mile east of the shaft show similar mineralization, which also was noted in narrow veins parallel to the schistosity.

These workings are apparently on the ground formerly held as the Jackson claims (no. 25, fig. 11), which were described by Chapin [27] and Mertie [28] in 1913 and 1916. In 1916 several open cuts and shafts and a tunnel 516 feet long had been driven. The vein was of particular interest because of its unusually heavy concentration of sul-

[26] Smith, P. S., op. cit. (Bull. 525), pp. 182–185.
[27] Chapin, Theodore, op. cit. (Bull. 592), p. 338.
[28] Mertie, J. B., Jr., op. cit. (Bull. 662), pp. 416–447.

phides, including pyrite, arsenopyrite, stibnite, and jamesonite, as well as gold and silver. Apparently these claims have lain idle for years.

CLEARY HILL

The Cleary Hill Alaska Gold Mines Co. acquired, about 1924, the formerly highly productive Rhoads-Hall mine and adjacent claims (no. 15, fig. 11) covering the point of the ridge between Chatham and Bedrock Creeks, tributaries of Cleary Creek. The Free Gold claim is the only one of the 11 claims in the group that has been patented. It was patented under mineral survey 821, dated August 13, 1913. The group as shown on plate 4 consists of the Free Gold, Snowdrift, New York, Texas, California, Pauper's Dream, Idaho, Colorado, and a half interest in the Wyoming and Wyoming Fraction, the claims covering approximately 200 acres of mineralized ground. The Gustafson brothers are in charge of the mine, which is sometimes known by their name. The mill and camp on the west end of the Free Gold claim are 25 miles by a good automobile road northeast of Fairbanks and about 2 miles southwest of Cleary post office. The main power line of the Fairbanks Exploration Co. passes about three quarters of a mile north of the camp. (See pl. 3.)

The Cleary Hill mine is currently reported to have produced over $1,000,000, most of which came from the stoped ground near the surface above the big fault that crosses the Penrose tunnel about 200 feet from the portal (see pl. 5) and was taken out by Rhoads and Hall, the discoverers. This was one of the first producing lode mines in the Fairbanks district, and its mill was built in 1911. The present mill has five stamps of 1,000 pounds each and a 7 by 9 inch crusher of the Blake type, operated by a 100-horsepower Washington-Diesel engine, which also runs a 9 by 12 inch air compressor and a generator for lighting the mine, mill, and camp. The Diesel engine was installed in 1931 and is reported to have cut the cost of milling very materially as compared with the coal-burning steam plant formerly in use. There is a well-equipped blacksmith shop with Ingersoll-Rand drill sharpener and waste-oil furnace in the mill building. At one time there was a concentrating table in the mill, but this was not in place in September 1931. It is reported [29] that the capacity of the mill will be increased in the near future.

The Cleary Hill vein strikes N. 70°–80° W. and dips 43°–60° S., averaging about 50°. It is situated approximately on the crest of the low anticline, along which the major mineralization of the Pedro Dome region appears to have occurred. As a consequence of this

---

[29] Eng. and Min. Jour., vol. 132, p. 423, Nov. 9, 1931.

situation, the vein is broken by an intricate system of faults. Those
with the greatest throw are practically parallel to the vein but dip
north instead of south. The original workings were all to the west
of and above such a fault, which is well shown in the main level just
east of the winze. This zone is between 30 and 40 feet wide and consists of crushed contorted schist and gouge that strikes N. 75° E.
and dips 45°–60° NNW. Heavy slickensides on many slip planes
show most of the movement to have been nearly horizontal or with
low dips either east or west. A similar fault zone known as the
"Brandell fault " is shown near the "island " in the no. 1 tunnel
level, where the raise from the Penrose tunnel comes up. This fault
zone strikes N. 70° E. and dips 80° NNW. On the level of the no. 1
tunnel there is about 30 feet of heavy ground, and exposures are
poor. A third fault of this character is seen near the face of the
Penrose tunnel level. The fault zone here, known as the "Wyer
fault ", strikes N. 70° W. and dips 45° SSW. The vein has not been
found beyond this fault. There is about 40 feet of crushed schist
and gouge in the zone, with several major slip planes marked by
slickensides that indicate nearly horizontal movement. Movement
on these large faults seems to have been reversed, so far as the veins
are concerned, though the movement was essentially horizontal. The
throw varied from about 75 feet on the Brandell fault to nearly 170
feet on the Front fault shown in the main workings.

Besides the faults mentioned above there is a closely spaced series
of north-south planes of movement that strike from N. 20° E. to
N. 20° W. and dip either east or west at relatively steep angles.
Movement along this series has been normal in every case, and a fair
rule has been worked out for picking up segments of the veins beyond
a fault—that is, when going east on the vein, if a fault dips west the
vein will be picked up to the south; if the fault dips east the segment
will be found to the north.

A third series of faults occurs approximately parallel to the schistosity of the enclosing rocks. This series strikes approximately east,
ranging between N. 70° W. and N. 70° E. and dips in general 5° to
15° either north or south. In several places where such faults were
noted and could be studied in detail the movement was found to be
reverse, with a throw of only a few feet, or in some places of only a
few inches. In some stopes above the main tunnel level the segments
beyond these relatively flat faults have not been found, but in others
they have been; the best example of a place where the segment has
been found is in the raise and winze connecting the Penrose and no. 1
tunnel levels near the east end of the workings, where the offset was
only 1 foot.

As will be seen from plate 5 the workings are extensive and intricate, owing to the complex faulting of the vein. Development costs are proportionately high, especially as the vein is only 4 to 24 inches wide, averaging 12 inches. Fortunately the ore is rich, samples taken by the writer indicating an average value of $33.40 a ton. Mill heads have been maintained at around $40 a ton for the last few years, thanks in part to an exceptionally rich body of ore in the bank stope on the no. 1 tunnel level east of the Goessmann shaft.

The vein as exposed in the various levels and stopes is very similar throughout, consisting of crushed and recemented quartz, which is generally free from both walls and iron-stained. The richer ore has a peculiar yellowish-green stain that is probably due to the presence of a mixture of scorodite and antimony oxide. Free gold is visible in much of the ore. It usually occurs with minor quantities of arsenopyrite and still less stibnite. Sulphides were present even in ores from pits on the surface east of the Windlass shaft and in oxidized ore at the face of the main tunnel along fractures in the vein. It is clearly evident, however, that the gold in the part of the vein now being worked is primary and accompanied the deposition of sulphides in one of the latest stages of the mineralization.

It is difficult to arrive at even an approximate estimate of the quantity of ore opened in the last few years in the Cleary Hill mine, because of the uncertainties as to the size and distribution of the vein segments that have been dislocated through faulting. Nevertheless, it is believed that a considerable tonnage has been indicated by the development, though it cannot be classed as ore that has been blocked by openings on three sides. It is estimated that at least 1,800 tons has been indicated between the Penrose and no. 1 tunnel level east of the Bank stope and that there is an additional 3,500 tons of probable ore having a value of at least $25 a ton between no. 1 tunnel and the surface. There is also little doubt that 2,700 tons of ore occurs in the two veins exposed on the main tunnel up to the Penrose level. On the basis of the above figures, 8,000 tons of ore containing about $200,000 in gold may be considered as partly blocked out, and there is a strong likelihood that this property may contain an additional 50,000 tons of ore of comparable richness.

On the surface east of the Jones raise and the Windlass shaft there is a major fault striking apparently north, though the relations are not entirely clear. This is the Goessmann vein, which was productive in the early days of quartz mining but which has not been worked for some years. East of this fault a vein with approximately the strike of the Cleary Hill vein has been exposed in a series of open cuts and pits for at least 300 feet. A sample from one of the pits near the east end of the work on the Chatham Creek slope taken across 14 inches assayed $30.60 to the ton.

Three claims now incorporated into the holdings of the Cleary Hill mine—namely, the California, Pauper's Dream, and Texas—were described in some detail by Smith.[30] These claims are not now being developed.

WYOMING

The Wyoming or Wackwitz mine (no. 14, fig. 11) consists of the Oklahoma, Wackwitz placer, and Wyoming claims. The Gustafson brothers own a half interest in the Wyoming claim. This group lies immediately south of the Cleary Hill mine, on the east side of Bedrock Creek. The camp and mill are at an elevation of 1,175 feet about 50 feet above the creek level and half a mile south of Cleary Creek. There is a small jawcrusher and a 3 by 4 foot Herman ball mill, run by an automobile gasoline engine, at the mouth of the lower tunnel. It has been used for mill testing of the ores. This vein has produced several thousand dollars' worth of ore but can hardly be said to have been more than prospected.

The main development is through two tunnels about 70 feet apart vertically, only the lower one of which was open in September 1931, as the upper Wyoming tunnel was caved at the mouth. The lower tunnel runs east for about 300 feet along a vein striking N. 80° E. and dipping 50° S., to a fault that strikes a little west of north and dips 45° W. East of this fault two veins have been opened. What appears to be the Wyoming vein was shifted about 100 feet south by the fault. (See fig. 13.) The vein cannot be seen near the mouth of the lower tunnel, as it has been iced up. At raise A, west of the fault, the vein is 12 inches wide, and the ore has been stoped up to a flat fault 30 feet above the level. Movement on this fault was horizontal and produced 3 feet of crushed schist. Beyond the north-south fault a drift was turned east on a narrow quartz vein striking S. 80° E. and dipping 35° S. This vein is from 2 to 4 inches wide but in places splits into stringers of quartz, several of which occur in a width of 12 to 14 inches at the face of the north drift. In a 15-foot crosscut north from the face there are two stringers of quartz that are well mineralized. The schist in this vicinity is more or less silicified and contains some pyrite. It should be more thoroughly prospected, as the ore and altered wall rock resemble some of the ore at the Tolovana mine, which is known to be rich.

The main vein was cut in a south crosscut east of the fault about 100 feet south of its projection and has been followed eastward by a drift for 200 feet. One stope 70 feet long had been carried

---

[30] Smith, P. S., op. cit. (Bull. 525), pp. 180–182.

through to the upper tunnel, and a raise about 75 feet from the
face has been put through for ventilation. The vein in the stope
near the fault dips 50° S. and is from 12 to 14 inches wide. It consists of hard, solid white quartz. In the stopes near the raise the
vein averaged 12 inches in width but in places contained as much
as 3 feet of crushed vein filling consisting of gouge, silicified schist,

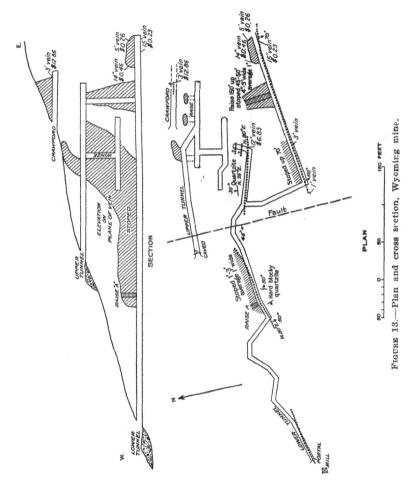

FIGURE 13.—Plan and cross section, Wyoming mine.

and quartz. A 1 to 2 inch streak of well-mineralized quartz follows the hanging wall. This ore is said to have milled more than
$6 a ton. The stope above the face of the tunnel is on the vein,
which here ranges from 15 inches of solid quartz to 5 feet of crushed
schist and quartz, all more or less iron-stained and mineralized. In
places the quartz splits into several small stringers, which reunite
to form a solid vein within a few feet along either the strike or the

dip. Samples cut by the writer in this stope showed only low values, though panning tests gave good results.

The Crawford tunnel, up the hill east-northeast of the mill was driven on a vein that dips north instead of south. It consists of seven stringers of quartz from half an inch to 1 inch wide in a zone 3 feet wide, with some pyrite in the silicified quartzite schist between the stringers. A sample cut across the 3 feet gave assays of $12.86 to the ton.

A new tunnel which will run a little south of east is being started by the Wackwitz brothers near the level of Bedrock Creek. It should cut the vein found in the Crawford tunnel in a relatively short distance but will have to be driven several hundred feet to reach the Wyoming vein.

There is very little ore actually blocked out in the Wyoming mine so far as could be seen, but the probability of future work disclosing considerable ore is regarded as good.

B.P.

The inclined shaft and tunnels of the B.P. claim (no. 10, fig. 11), on the west side of Chatham Creek half a mile above Cleary Creek, were inaccessible in 1931 and could not be examined. The vein apparently strikes N. 85° E. and dips 45° S. Material on the dump is a bluish silicified schist with some quartz and a large amount of gouge. A 4-foot Herman ball mill is on the ground but was not installed for operation.

This property was extensively prospected between 1908 and 1912, and Prindle [31] reports that in 1909 it was developed by a tunnel 90 feet long from which a winze 150 feet deep was sunk on a shear zone, and a raise was made to the surface. From the shaft a 40-foot drift was made in each direction along the shear zone at a point 100 feet below the main level. The shear zone was impregnated with sulphides, chiefly pyrite and arsenopyrite, but with some galena, sphalerite, and stibnite. Free gold was found in the upper, more oxidized portions of the mineralized zone but was not recognized in the lower portion.

SCOTT REESE

The Scott Reese tunnel (no. 9, fig. 11) is on the west side of Chatham Creek about 200 feet south of the old B.P. workings. This tunnel runs westward through schists, which dip 30°–40° N. The tunnel is 320 feet long and intersects a 4-inch fault zone 20 feet from the mouth, a 3-inch quartz vein 150 feet from the mouth, and

---

[31] Prindle, L. M., Auriferous quartz veins in the Fairbanks district: U.S. Geol. Survey Bull. 442, p. 226, 1910.

a well-defined fault striking N. 60° E. and dipping 80° S. about 230 feet from the mouth. At the face there is a 1-inch quartz vein. This tunnel was driven to intercept a vein exposed in some pits on the surface but had not reached its objective in the middle of July 1931.

PIONEER

The Pioneer mine (no. 8, fig. 11), on Chatham Creek less than a mile above its mouth, deserves mention because it was here that the first gold quartz claim in the Fairbanks district was located in 1903, as the Blue Bell lode.

The old shaft house and mill, on the east side of Chatham Creek, are now gone, and the property is now abandoned. Prindle,[32] who visited the property in 1909, reports that two shafts, one 24 feet and the other 85 feet deep, had been sunk on a vein about 3 feet thick, with a smaller intersecting vein, both of which carried free gold. In succeeding years a 5-stamp mill was constructed and several hundred tons of ore was milled. Apparently no work has been done on this property for many years.

ALASKA

A group of three claims called the "Alaska group " was located by F. M. Wackwitz on the east side of Chatham Creek in 1931. They cover the old Jupiter-Mars ground (no. 6, fig. 11) in part and extend from the Chatham mine patented ground to Chatham Creek just above the Chatham mill. The old Jupiter-Mars workings are caved and inaccessible. They are reported to include two tunnels and a shaft 125 feet deep with 112 feet of drifts. The work on the new claims consists largely of long ditches that have been sluiced through the surface material and several shallow pits. A pit near the center of the center claim shows the top of a badly crushed and heavily oxidized quartz vein. As indicated by the float this vein is from 3 to 5 feet thick and near the surface seems to dip about 30° N. and strikes about east. A grab sample from the dump assayed 43 cents to the ton, but much of the material has the characteristic greenish-yellow arsenic stain indicative of ore carrying considerable gold.

At the center of the easternmost claim there are two or three small veins that strike N. 50°–60° E. which come into the east-west vein. One of these stringers exposed in a 10-foot shaft is 8 to 10 inches wide and assayed $16.88 to the ton. Another vein near the east end of this claim strikes N. 45° E. and dips 50° SE. The vein is 18 inches wide and consists of promising-looking iron-stained quartz and crushed schist. It is said that Foster and Hungerford worked

---

[32] Prindle, L. M., op. cit. (Bull 442), p. 226.

this vein in 1913 and 1914 and took out a few tons of $40 ore from an open cut.

Nils Genki has a claim covering part of the north end of the old Jupiter-Mars ground. There is a shallow shaft, which could not be entered, on a vein that strikes N. 60° E. and appears to be from 10 to 12 inches wide. The quartz is crushed and stained with both iron and arsenic oxides, indicative of good ore.

ANNA-MARY

J. O. Warren, in 1931, was prospecting on the point of the hill between Chatham and Tamarack Creeks (no. 7, fig. 11) and had opened two lodes. The Mary lode strikes N. 70° W. and dips 70° S. It is reached by several shallow shafts along the strike, is from 4 to 8 feet wide, and consists of 1 to 6 feet of crushed schist on the hanging wall and 1 to 2 feet of blue clay gouge on the footwall. Lenticular masses of badly crushed iron-stained quartz were noted in some places, and galena and arsenopyrite high in silver were seen in samples on the dump. A sample cut across 5 feet of this material at the bottom of a 15-foot shaft assayed 46 cents to the ton. The Anna lode lies about 100 feet south of the Mary and up the hill but had not been opened sufficiently in July 1931 to permit any conclusive observations as to its strike or character.

CHATHAM

The workings of the Chatham mine (no. 4, fig. 11) are at the head of Chatham Creek at an elevation of 1,800 feet. The ground is patented under mineral survey 1713, dated August 6-11, 1923, and consists of a compact group of five claims known as the Chatham No. 2, Fay, Colby, Colby No. 2, and Fay No. 2, covering 97 acres. The Chatham Mining Co. was a local organization, which is now largely controlled by Mrs. William Burns, of Fairbanks. The Chatham mill is on the west side of Chatham Creek about 2 miles below the mine, this site having been selected in order to obtain an adequate supply of water. This mine has produced considerable gold in the past but has not been active of late. The mill buildings are in bad repair, and part of the machinery has been removed. There is a 7 by 9 inch crusher of the Blake type, and 2 batteries of 2 stamps each, which are still in good condition.

All the surface pits at the Chatham mine had caved, and when visited on July 8, 1931, the main tunnel was so iced up that it could not be entered. This main tunnel, which has been driven as a crosscut, trends N. 30° E. and intersects the vein at a point about 200 feet from the portal. All that could be seen was the top of the caved stopes, which indicate that the vein strikes about N. 70° W.

As described in some detail by Smith,[33] in 1912, several hundred feet of drifts had been driven along the vein, stopes had been opened, and considerable ore extracted. Apparently the mine was operated for a few years as a gold mine, but in 1916, according to Mertie,[34] it was worked for the antimony ore which it contained. At that time the main tunnel was 1,300 feet long, raises and winzes had been driven, and antimony ore was being taken out both above and below the main tunnel level.

At present this mine is inactive.

HOMESTAKE

The Homestake (Nordale) patented claims (no. 1, fig. 11) are on the west fork of Wolf Creek near its head. The claims, which were surveyed in June 1928, under mineral survey 1607, are the Wolf, Keystone, Kawalita, Fairbanks, and Hope. (See pl. 6.) They belong to the Nordale estate, of Fairbanks, Alton Nordale, agent, and apparently include the ground formerly owned by both the Homestake and the Rexall mines.

The principal development is a crosscut tunnel whose mouth is at an elevation of 1,500 feet near the creek. The tunnel runs south along the center line of the group for about 350 feet to a vein that strikes N. 70° E. and dips 40° S. This vein, where cut, shows 2 to 3 inches of white quartz, very distinct from the surrounding black mica schists, which here lie practically horizontal. Drifts were turned both ways on this vein, and the crosscut continued south. Owing to bad caving at the vein crossing it was not possible to penetrate beyond this point in 1931. It is said that the crosscut has a total length of 800 feet and intersects one more vein about 400 feet from the face. Mr. Nordale stated that about $60,000 had been taken from stopes on the narrow vein nearest the mouth of the tunnel. According to Mr. Henderson, who at present is operating the Mohawk mine, on Ester Dome, but who earlier operated the Homestake under lease, the narrow vein was extremely rich in spots but had never been worked below the tunnel level because of the heavy flow of water. At one time there was a stamp mill just northeast of the tunnel mouth, but this had been removed before July 1931.

A lower tunnel on the Fairbanks claim a short distance northeast of the crosscut and 50 feet lower was caved 60 feet from the mouth. It appeared to follow an eastward-trending vein. About 100 feet above the mouth of the crosscut and a little east of south, is the dump of a tunnel which is caved at the mouth. This mine was described in some detail by Smith [35] and Chapin,[36] but is at present inactive.

[33] Smith, P. S., op. cit. (Bull. 525), pp. 172–173.
[34] Mertie, J. B., Jr., op. cit. (Bull. 662), p. 415.
[35] Smith, P. S., op. cit. (Bull. 525), p. 168.
[36] Chapin, Theodore, op. cit. (Bull. 592), pp. 331–334.

As shown on plate 6, the Homestake group of claims includes the ground formerly known as the "Rexall mine." The Rexall mine was not studied in 1931 but has been described at some length by Smith [37] and Chapin.[38] It was developed by a tunnel 140 feet long driven along a quartz vein to the intersection of another vein, to which subsequent work was confined. A drift was carried along this vein for 500 feet, raises and winzes were driven, and stopes opened from which ore was taken. The ore was essentially quartz, with few sulphides, and some ore of exceptionally high value was recovered. A 2-stamp mill, with crusher, operated by a gasoline engine, was built in 1912. This mine was not in operation in 1917 and apparently has been idle since that time.

M'CARTY

F. J. McCarty owns a group of 10 claims on the divide between Fairbanks Creek and the head of Wolf Creek, just north of the Henry Ford group. (See pl. 6.) This group includes the Marigold, I. B., Harrietta, Pioneer, Willie, Pennsylvania, Free Gold, Laughing Water, Minnie Ha-Ha, and Henry Clay claims. A great deal of surface prospecting has been done on these claims on seven veins. The greatest amount of development has been done on the Pioneer vein (no. 2, fig. 14), near Mr. McCarty's house, and on the Pennsylvania vein on the Wolf Creek side of the divide. The Pioneer vein strikes N. 65° W. and dips 60° S. Some antimony ore was shipped from a shallow shaft on the Antimony vein, which is about half-way between the main road and Mr. McCarty's house, directly on the saddle. The production from the Pioneer vein is stated by Mr. McCarty to have been $14,000 from ore taken out above the 50-foot level in the shafts immediately east of his house. This work was all caved and inaccessible early in July 1931 and was not examined.

As described by Smith,[39] in 1912, the Pioneer claim was developed by one shaft 110 feet deep, with drifts about 200 feet long to both the east and the west, a second shaft 75 feet deep east of the main shaft, a 38-foot shaft still farther east, and many open pits, a total distance of 800 feet. In addition, several other veins had been discovered on this group of claims.

The Pennsylvania claim was developed by a shaft, said to be 146 feet deep but now full of water, on a vein that strikes N. 80° E. and dips 60°–70° S. This vein has been stoped to a width of 18 inches for 60 to 70 feet west of the shaft, to a depth of 50 feet, and is said to have yielded about $10,000 worth of gold.

[37] Smith, P. S., op. cit. (Bull. 525), pp. 168–170.
[38] Chapin, Theodore, op. cit. (Bull. 592), pp. 334–335.
[39] Smith, P. S., op. cit. (Bull. 525), p. 164.

It is reported that a vein that extends from the Pioneer claim eastward into adjoining ground contains stibnite in places to a thickness of 8 inches.

There is no equipment of any sort on the McCarty ground, and as none of the workings were accessible, no estimate of possible tonnage can be made. There are, however, excellent surface showings of ore, and the property deserves thorough investigation along systematic lines.

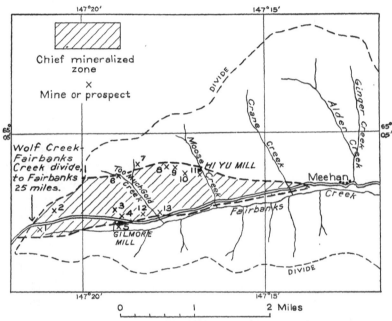

FIGURE 14.—Map of Fairbanks Creek drainage basin, showing location of mines and prospects described in this report.

1. Henry Ford.	7–11. Hi-Yu:	12. Plumbum.
2. Pioneer.	7. Dorando shaft.	13. Bishop.
3. Mizpah.	8. Upper shaft.	
4. Ohio.	9. Upper tunnel.	
5. Gilmore tunnel and mill.	10. Middle tunnel.	
6. McNeil.	11. Lower (mill) tunnel.	

FAIRBANKS CREEK

Fairbanks Creek has been a rich placer stream, as were its tributaries from the north. So far as could be learned, little or no gold was derived from the short southern tributaries, and prospecting for lodes south of the creek has not been successful. The belt of lode mines is shown in figure 14. It is said that a few prospects of promise were found near the heads of Alder and Walnut Creeks, north of Meehan, and that at one time a little ore was taken from prospects on the north side of Coffee Dome, at the head of Kokomo Creek, but these workings have been abandoned for years and were not examined.

In 1931 the Hi-Yu mine was producing and some ore was being taken out on the American Eagle vein of the Henry Ford group (no. 1, fig. 14). None of the other lode properties in Fairbanks Creek were being developed.

Northeast of the mouth of Too Much Gold Creek are some old caved workings on a vein striking N. 70° W. that is said to be about 2 feet wide. This was mentioned by Smith as the Whitehorse mine. It was said to be held by Frank Bishop in 1931.

West of Bishop's cabin at the mouth of Too Much Gold Creek are the abandoned shaft and cuts on what was formerly known as the Plumbum claim. The surface showings indicate that the vein strikes N. 70° W. and dips 70° S.

The Michael McNeil shaft is at the head of the west fork of Too Much Gold Creek a little below the summit of the divide to Wolf Creek, at an elevation of 2,250 feet. The shaft was iced up and the tunnel caved at the mouth, and the surface pits on the divide to the northwest were also inaccessible. The vein apparently strikes N. 60° W. and dips 70° S. The country rock is light-colored quartz-mica schist. A little ore that was found in sacks in the nearly wrecked cabin on the claim consisted of quartz, arsenopyrite, jamesonite, and galena.

HENRY FORD

The Henry Ford group of six full claims lies at the head of Fairbanks Creek, just east of the Wolf Creek divide at an elevation of 1,900 to 2,200 feet. L. J. McCarty owns a three-quarter interest and the estate of George Ewers a quarter interest in these claims. The group consists of the Henry Ford, Henry Ford No. 1, Henry Ford No. 2, Henry Ford No. 3, Henry Ford No. 4, and Golden Eagle claims. The Henry Ford is a relocation covering the old American Eagle property.

During 1929 and 1930 the shaft on the McCarty vein on the Henry Ford No. 3 claim was sunk 50 feet and the vein stoped to that depth for a total distance of 450 feet. (See fig. 15.) During this period, according to the operator, 1,225 tons of ore was taken out and milled at the Gilmore mill, a mile east on Fairbanks Creek, yielding $26,770 in bullion, or more than $21.50 a ton. At this shaft there is a light timber gallows frame, a ½-ton skip, and a 6-horsepower Fairbanks-Morse gasoline-driven hoist. All drilling was done by hand, and there is a good supply of drill steel in the blacksmith shop, which is well equipped. Several hundred feet of light rails are also available.

The McCarty vein strikes N. 78° W. and dips 75° S. It is opened by a 60-foot inclined shaft on the dip of the vein and is near the west center of the claim, about one eighth of a mile south of the main road on the saddle at the head of Fairbanks Creek. The timbers at the 50-foot station had given way in July 1931, and the drift west on the vein was caved at the shaft so that it could not be entered. As shown on the plan (fig. 15), this level is about 370 feet long and intersected two cross veins about 200 and 250 feet west of the shaft, which are offset by the McCarty vein. These cross veins, which strike about N. 40° E. and dip southeast at steep angles, are opened by shallow prospect pits and have not been further developed. The plan shows that the vein was cut off by a fault and not picked up at the west end of the 60-foot level. The east drift had been driven 170 feet but was inaccessible beyond a point near the shaft because of caving. Near the cave the vein was seen in a pillar.

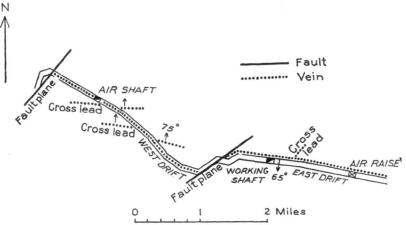

FIGURE 15.—Plan of 60-foot level, Henry Ford No. 3 shaft, McCarty property.

It consists of 30 inches of quartz next to the hanging wall with 30 to 35 inches of crushed quartz, schist, and gouge above the footwall slip. Slickensides on the hanging wall show postmineral horizontal movement, which verifies the mapping of the offset of the cross veins in the west drift. If the statement of tonnage taken out above the 50-foot level is correct it indicates that the vein averaged a little over 1 foot in width. One sample of badly crushed iron-stained quartz from a pillar of the hanging-wall streak 30 inches wide, at a point 50 feet from the shaft, assayed 66 cents to the ton.

The next largest development on this group is the American Eagle tunnel, which starts at the south end of the Henry Ford claim near the creek level at an elevation of about 1,975 feet. (See pl. 6.) This tunnel was caved at the mouth in July 1931 and could not be examined. It is said to have been driven on the vein which strikes approximately N. 70° W., for about 500 feet. There are several caved shafts on the vein farther northwest, up the hill, and in September 1931 Mr. McCarty had opened the vein again near the summit, just below the road, in a series of pits and shafts. One of these shafts near the north end of the claim and 250 feet below the road was 25 feet deep. The vein here strikes N. 70° W. and dips 72° S. At the bottom of the shaft a drift 8 feet long had been turned off to the west. The vein at the face was 24 inches wide and consisted of crushed quartz and gouge which assayed $13.66 a ton. At the time of the writer's visit, in September 1931, the first round had just been shot on the east drift, and the vein there consisted of 10 inches of quartz next to the hanging wall with 18 to 24 inches of crushed quartz and mineralized gouge below. Postmineral movement along the vein was very pronounced, and the striae are horizontal or dip slightly to the west. In the course of sinking this shaft about 10 tons of ore had been saved for milling. A grab sample of the ore pile gave an assay of $16.06 a ton. In some of the pits between the new shaft described above and the mouth of the tunnel the vein was from 10 to 30 inches wide, and some high-grade ore had been exposed. The total production from this vein, according to Mr. McCarty, has been $15,000, from ore that ran between $12 and $70 a ton. The best ore came from the shaft near the center of the claim.

The so-called Big vein or Upper and Lower Henry Ford veins (see pl. 6) appear to be two parts of the same vein which has been faulted along the American Eagle vein. The segment west of the American Eagle vein is called on the map the Upper Henry Ford vein. It is exposed in several pits, which were badly caved in 1931 but nevertheless show a vein from 4 to 5 feet in width of iron-stained crushed quartz with a rather larger proportion of sulphides than is usual in the Fairbanks district. Two grab samples of ore from two different pits assayed $15.69 and $18.98 to the ton. The segment east of the American Eagle vein has been traced for 600 feet by surface pits. The last one of these to the east was 10 feet deep and exposed a vein striking N. 30° E. and dipping 75° NW. This vein consisted of crushed iron-stained quartz and gouge and is said to average $12 a ton. A sample cut over a width of 4 feet assayed $3.62. The average of all the samples taken by the writer on the Henry Ford vein gave a width of 4 feet 4 inches and a value of $12.99 a ton.

As shown on plate 6 there are several other veins exposed by surface trenches and pits on the Henry Ford group, but no sinking has been done on them. On the whole this property is fairly well prospected on the surface, with every indication that it should be worked much more extensively. Although there is practically no developed ore in sight, there is reason to believe that it is an exceptionally good prospect that warrants development.

MIZPAH

The Mizpah property (no. 3, fig. 14) is on the ridge north of Fairbanks Creek about 1½ miles east of the Wolf Creek summit and 1 mile west-northwest of the mouth of Too Much Gold Creek. The property belongs to Charles Thompson, who was not in Alaska during the summer of 1931. The number of claims held in this property is not known to the writer.

The main inclined shaft, at an elevation of 1,750 feet, is sunk on a vein striking N. 65° W. and dipping 70° S. It is equipped with a small wood-burning steam boiler and a marine-type steam hoist of about 10 horsepower. The shaft was accessible only as far as the 80-foot level, 50 feet below which it had caved, and the west drift on the 80-foot level was open to the face, a distance from the shaft of about 120 feet. The drift to the east was caved 50 feet from the shaft, as were the stopes on each side of the shaft to the surface. The vein as exposed in a few pillars in the western drift on the 80-foot level is from 20 to 24 inches wide and consists of crushed iron-stained quartz. At the face of the drift no quartz was seen. The crushed schist filling the fracture assayed $2.30 to the ton over a width of 16 inches. Specimens found on the dump show the ore to be siliceous, badly crushed, and but little iron-stained.

It is reported that the Gilmore tunnel, which has its portal between the road and Fairbanks Creek at an elevation of 1,650 feet, about half a mile above the mouth of Too Much Gold Creek, connects with the Mizpah shaft and that a considerable tonnage of fair-grade ore was mined above this level from the Mizpah vein.

This mine has produced a small quantity of rich ore. The average value of all that has been mined is reported to be between $30 and $40 a ton.

OHIO

The Ohio group of claims (no. 4, fig. 14) lies along the north slope of Fairbanks Creek west of Too Much Gold Creek and east of the Mizpah lode. This ground was described by Mertie [40] in 1916, when development of the property was active. He reports that shafts had been sunk on several quartz veins, but that in order to prospect the ground better a crosscut tunnel 800 feet long was being driven, of which 240 feet were completed. Five shafts then open ranged from 25 to 70 feet in depth and disclosed veins of varying value and thickness. In 1915 the Gilmore mill, a 5-stamp mill, was erected by the owners of the Ohio group, and 350 tons of ore taken from that ground was milled.

[40] Mertie, J. B., Jr., op. cit. (Bull. 662), pp. 408–409.

In 1931 all the workings on this property were either full of ice or caved and therefore inaccessible. The property has not been actively mined for some years.

GILMORE

The Gilmore mill, on Fairbanks Creek (no. 5, fig. 14), is just below the automobile road about 1½ miles east of the Fairbanks-Wolf Creek divide at an elevation of 1,650 feet. The equipment consists of a 7 by 9 inch crusher of the Blake type, a 5-stamp Allis-Chalmers battery, and a 4 by 16 foot plate, operated by a 10-horsepower engine. There is a 40-horsepower coal-burning boiler which supplies steam for the mill engine and pump, located over a well in the mill building. For the last 2 years this mill has been leased to L. J. McCarty, who has used it to treat ore from the Henry Ford group of mines.

The tunnel starts at the surface at a point on a level with the top of the mill and had been driven N. 30° W. for a distance of 450 feet. Beyond this point the ground is caved, so that the continuation of the tunnel could not be examined, but it is said to connect with both the Ohio and Mizpah mine workings. The schists cut by the tunnel dip 10°–15° N.

A small compressor and gasoline engine installed at the mouth of the tunnel are said to belong to Charles Thompson, owner of the Mizpah mine.

HI-YU

The Hi-Yu or Crites & Feldman mine (nos. 7 to 11, fig. 14) is a consolidation of most of the claims on the ridge between Moose and Too Much Gold Creeks. The camp and mill are on Moose Creek about half a mile north of Fairbanks Creek, 4 miles west of Meehan, the nearest post office, and 27 miles northeast of Fairbanks by a good automobile road. The group consists of eight claims (fig. 16), none of which are patented, though a large amount of work has been done on them. They are the Yankee Doodle Fraction, Helen S., Teddy R., Insurgent, Hi-Yu, Summit, Dorando, and Sunnyside. The group trends in a northwesterly direction from the mill on Moose Creek to the head of Too Much Gold Creek, a total length of 7,000 feet. In this distance a series of at least three nearly parallel veins have been opened on the surface by many cuts and pits. The property belongs to Henry Feldman and the Crites estate, but in 1931 it was under a 5-year lease to Mr. Feldman, who with his partner had been operating the mine continuously since 1913.

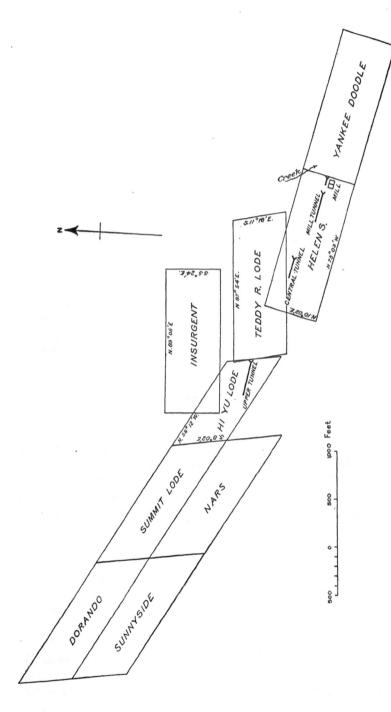

Figure 16.—Claim map, Hi-Yu mine.

This property was one of the first in the Fairbanks district to have its own mill. The main mill, which is on Moose Creek at an elevation of 1,680 feet, has a 7 by 9 inch jawcrusher of Blake type, five stamps, weighing 1,250 pounds each, and a 5 by 12 foot plate. It is driven by a steam engine supplied by a coal-burning boiler. The mill building is of good construction, and a well for winter mill water is located just outside but sufficiently covered so that it does not freeze. The total production by this mill prior to 1931 was about $252,000 from 8,200 tons of ore, indicating a mill recovery of approximately $32 a ton. Part of the tailings have been stored behind a rock and moss dam in Moose Creek. Assays indicate an average content of $4.18 a ton for this tailings material. The exact quantity of tailings that have been impounded was not determined, but it is probably only a few hundred tons. In 1931 Mr. Feldman installed a Gibson rod mill at the mouth of the center or main tunnel (see pl. 7) and moved the crusher to the new mill. This mill is driven by a 10-horsepower Fairbanks-Morse gasoline motor. The mill building is of frame construction covered with insulite and houses also a 12 by 10 inch Ingersoll-Rand compressor, run by a separate 15-horsepower gasoline motor, and the blacksmith shop, which has an Ingersoll-Rand drill sharpener. There is a complete assay equipment in a separate building near the old mill and a well-appointed camp for 10 to 12 men on the east side of Moose Creek opposite the mill.

The principal development is on the Helen S.-Teddy R. vein in four adit tunnels aggregating 3,600 feet of lateral work, besides several crosscuts and about 2,000 feet of raises and winzes. The lower tunnel, just below the mill on Moose Creek, was iced up about 300 feet from the mouth, and the mill tunnel was caved at the mouth, so they could not be examined in 1931. The main working tunnel, at an elevation of 1,950 feet on the west side of Moose Creek, follows the Helen S. vein for 1,200 feet and then by a short crosscut to the north reaches the Hi-Yu vein, which has been followed for 300 feet. The upper tunnel on the Hi-Yu vein, at an elevation of 2,140 feet, was caved at the mouth. Entrance to a small portion of this tunnel was gained through the air shaft, whose collar is at an elevation of 2,210 feet. Westward from these main workings the Hi-Yu vein has been traced into the head of Too Much Gold Creek by a nearly continuous open cut. At the crest of the hill there was at one time a 75-foot shaft, now caved, and in the east head of Too Much Gold Creek there is a 100-foot inclined shaft on what appears to be the same vein. Besides the workings mentioned above there are a series of open cuts and shallow shafts on the west slope of Moose Creek on a parallel vein lying about 300 feet north of the Helen S. and Teddy R. outcrops. All these openings are badly caved and could not be examined. It is reported that the vein exposed by these workings averages from 30 to 50 inches in width and is of fair milling value throughout. Promising-appearing ore on several of the dumps seems to warrant further extensive prospecting and development.

The Helen S. vein as developed by the main tunnel has an average strike of about N. 65° W. but varies from N. 60° W. to N. 72° W. It stands practically vertical or with dips of 80°–85° S. Its width ranges from 4 to 30 inches and averages 10 to 12 inches. As shown by the cross section (pl. 7), two rather large stopes have been opened in that part of the Helen S. vein east of the big fault zone, and two on the north Hi-Yu vein west of this zone. Although it seems likely that the so-called north and south veins are in fact distinct, there is nevertheless the possibility that they may be parts of the same vein. The evidence for considering them separate veins lies in the differences in width, degree of crushing, and strike. The Helen S. vein strikes N. 65° W., whereas the Hi-Yu vein near the face of the tunnel strikes about N. 75° W. It appears wise to drive 1 or 2 crosscuts to the north from the main adit—one near the west end of the old stope on the south vein, and the other from a point close to the present mill-water sump. The samples taken by the writer indicate that the ore left in the south vein averages about $29 a ton. This value checks closely with the values disclosed by the stope record of 430 tons of $35 ore on the main level and 3,100 tons of $27 ore on the mill tunnel level. There is an unmined block of ground on this south vein above the main tunnel which is 300 feet long and has an average height of 140 feet. If an average width of the vein of 10 inches is assumed, this block contains 2,500 tons of $29 ore having a gross value of $72,500, which could be readily mined.

On the north Hi-Yu vein exposed at the far end of the main tunnel beyond the east-west fault, a block of 3,000 tons of $37 ore was taken from the upper tunnel and a block of 1,670 tons of $24 ore from the main tunnel. Samples taken by the writer from the stope just started above the main tunnel indicated that the ore averaged $10.63 a ton for an average width of 10 inches. If this vein between the upper and main tunnel and the air raise is regarded as blocked out (it is developed on three sides), there is in this block, which is 200 feet long by 190 feet high and 10 inches wide, 2,760 tons of ore, which at $10 a ton would have a value of $27,600; or if the average value of its ore should run as high as that from the two stoped areas—namely, $32.76—it would have a value of over $90,000.

There is every reason to believe that development on the mill tunnel will open at least 1,100 feet of vein with backs of 225 feet, which with an average width of 10 inches would give 14,700 tons of ore. If this ore maintains the average of $29 a ton indicated by the writer's samples, or of $31, the average of the stope on the middle level and the mill tunnel level, it would have a gross value between $426,000 and $455,700.

The vein opened by the upper tunnel has been extensively prospected by open cuts and shafts along the vein for at least 1,000 feet west of any deep development and has been shown to contain excellent ore. Grab samples taken from ore piled beside some of these openings assayed $8.82 and $23.38 a ton. There is good reason to expect that lateral development west of the present workings will be productive of much ore averaging more than $10 and probably nearly $15 a ton.

It is also believed that crosscuts should be driven north from the main tunnel to test the presence of the Hi-Yu vein within 50 to 70 feet of the Helen S. These crosscuts should be continued northward to cut the 30-inch vein shown by numerous pits on the surface to be about 300 feet north of the caved stopes on the Teddy R.-Helen S. system.

In the upper tunnel there is a suggestion that some of the schist, in a place where the vein has split around a 10-foot horse, may be sufficiently mineralized to constitute ore. This should be investigated, for it is possible that relatively large bodies of medium-grade ore may be found if examination of the mineralized wall rock is carried on systematically.

The fault problem as indicated by present developments is extremely simple, and none of the offsets noted on the surface to the west of the deep workings were more than 20 feet. The movement along all the faults seems to have been normal.

The mining of a narrow vein requires that some wall rock be broken to afford working room, but it is believed that this dilution need not interfere with successful operation.

The present milling practice is far from perfect, as it is estimated that there is a loss of nearly 20 percent of the mill-head value. No attempt is made to save the sulphides, which constitute about 1½ to 2 percent of the total ore, though panning tests and assays indicate that they carry at least $17.40 a ton in gold.

In summary, it is estimated that there is 5,200 tons of ore blocked out above the main tunnel which has a value between $100,000 and $163,000; that there is, between the mill tunnel and main tunnel, approximately 14,700 tons of probable ore having a value between $426,000 and $455,000; and that there is every reason to believe that development westward along the Hi-Yu vein and northward will open up much additional ore which it will pay to mine and mill.

The mineralogy of these veins is described in some detail by Smith,[41] who also gives an account of the progress of prospecting some other ground in the vicinity at the time of his visit in 1912.

GOLDSTREAM VALLEY

The most highly developed area of lodes in the Goldstream Valley is that on Twin Creek from Skoogy Gulch southwest for about 2

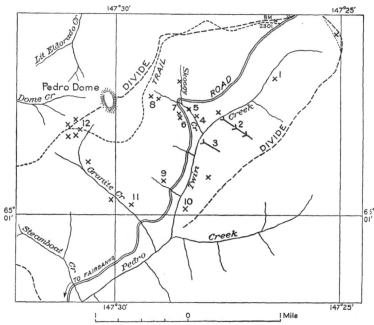

FIGURE 17.—Map of upper Goldstream Creek Valley, including Pedro, Twin, and Granite Creeks and Skoogy Gulch, showing location of mines and prospects described in this report.

1. White Elephant.	5. North Star (Big Lead).	9. Burnet Galena.
2. Moonlight.	6. David.	10. Zimmerman.
3. Harris.	7. North Star.	11. Birch & Anderson.
4. Rainbow.	8. Central Star.	12. Robinson.

miles and including Granite Creek, which joins Pedro Creek just below the mouth of Twin Creek. (See fig. 17.) The mineralization here evidently was closely associated with the intrusion of a coarse-grained granite porphyry mass at the mouth of Skoogy Gulch. This acidic rock intrudes both the Birch Creek schist and the fine-grained, more basic quartz diorite of Pedro Dome.

No ore was being produced at any of the properties in the Skoogy-Twin Creek area in 1931 and very little development or prospecting

[41] Smith, P. S., op. cit. (Bull. 525), pp. 156–157.

was in progress. Many of the surface workings were caved, and few of the shafts or tunnels could be entered.

WHITE ELEPHANT

The White Elephant tunnel (no. 1, fig. 17) at an elevation of 1,900 feet on the south side of Twin Creek, belonging to H. F. Faulkner, was caved in 1931 and could not be examined. Chapin,[42] who examined this property in 1913, says that a 20-foot tunnel was driven but had so caved that the relations in it were obscure. At this place flat lenses of galena are said to have occurred parallel with the foliation of the schist and associated with stringers of quartz. One of these bodies of galena measuring 9 by 5 feet and 5 inches thick was mined out, and the ore, which is reported to have carried considerable silver, was milled. A little pyrite occurs with the galena.

MOONLIGHT

The Moonlight group of three claims (no. 2, fig. 17) lies on the south side of Twin Creek a short distance above the mouth of Skoogy Gulch. All three tunnels and the connecting raises were in bad condition in July 1931. This work was done by Martin Harrais prior to 1913.

The lower tunnel was accessible in 1931 for the first 30 feet. It is driven S. 60° E. through coarse porphyritic granite to the schist contact in ground that is so badly caved at the contact that relations are not clear. The dump of this tunnel is mostly schist. The upper tunnel, entirely in quartz-mica schist, follows a fracture zone striking N. 75° E. that dips 75° N. It is accessible for 100 feet, and in that distance the vein is from 4 to 6 inches wide and consists of crushed quartz and schist with not much indication of mineralization. At 100 feet from the portal this tunnel is caved, but at that point what appeared to be the bottom of an ore shoot was noted. At the mouth of this tunnel there was a pile of about 3 tons of material that appears to have been saved as ore. A grab sample of this pile assayed $3.26 a ton.

No development work has recently been done on this property.

INDEPENDENCE

The Independence claim (no. 3, fig. 17) is on the southeast side of Twin Creek almost opposite the mouth of Skoogy Gulch. There are two tunnels on this lode. The lower, a few feet above Twin Creek, is iced up so that it could not be examined in 1931. Some specimens of narrow veinlets frozen to coarse porphyritic granite seen on the

---

[42] Chapin, Theodore, op. cit. (Bull. 592), p. 348.

dump carry high-grade free gold ore with a little arsenopyrite and pyrite. The upper tunnel, about 75 feet higher on the hill slope, has a length of about 50 feet. It shows several quartz veinlets in a zone 8 to 10 inches wide striking N. 70° E. and standing vertical in coarse-grained porphyritic granite. The veinlets are frozen to the wall rock. Coarse-grained pyrite and arsenopyrite are the chief metallic minerals in the vein. A sample taken across 6 inches of the zone assayed $6.86 to the ton. The vein is said to have been traced eastward to the top of the hill by a series of shallow pits, all of which were so badly caved in July 1931 that they did not afford evidence as to whether or not a vein was found in them.

RAINBOW AND DAVID

The Rainbow workings (no. 4, fig. 17) are on the point of the ridge between Twin Creek and Skoogy Gulch at an elevation of 1,700 feet. Both the old shaft and an adit tunnel whose mouth is in Skoogy Gulch were inaccessible on July 27, 1931. Apparently no mining had been done on the property for some time. The shaft is on the Rainbow claim, belonging to Nirige & Hershberger, and the mouth of the adit tunnel is on the David claim, of which one half is owned by the Northern Commercial Co. and one half by Drouin & Robinson.

The remains of a light 5-stamp Straube prospecting mill were seen near the old shaft, and a crusher and 2-stamp mill are located near the mouth of the adit on Skoogy Gulch.

Chapin,[48] who visited this property in 1913, reports that it was developed by a 100-foot shaft with a short drift on the 50-foot level and a 135-foot drift to the east and a 190-foot drift to the west on the 100-foot level. By 1913 about 480 tons of ore had been shipped and 45 tons had been milled on the property. This mine has made no production for a number of years.

The vein at the mouth of the adit, which beyond that point was iced up, appears to be about 1 foot wide and nearly vertical and to cut porphyritic granite and schist. East of the old shaft several shallow pits had been sunk, in which the vein had been traced as far as the valley fill in Twin Creek, nearly one eighth of a mile east of the shaft. A relatively new open cut just above the creek level exposes the vein well. Here the vein is seen to strike east and dip 85° S. It consists of 10 inches of white quartz with some arsenopyrite. On the footwall or south side is a 2-inch band of crushed heavily iron and manganese stained quartz which, upon panning, shows a concentrate of arsenopyrite and free gold. A sample cut across the whole 10 inches assayed $22.92 to the ton, and a sample of the 2-inch streak $212.14 to the ton.

---

[48] Chapin, Theodore, op. cit. (Bull. 592), p. 348.

On the west side of Skoogy Gulch the David tunnel (no. 6, fig. 17), which is 40 feet long, had been driven west on a vein that strikes N. 70° E. and dips 35° S. This vein is 22 inches wide, and samples from it assayed $1.04 and $1.24 a ton. The vein is exposed along the south side of the adit. Near the face of the tunnel there are two veins that strike west. The one on the south side of the tunnel is 1 inch wide at the roof of the tunnel and 4 inches at the floor. A sample taken in three cuts across this vein at roof, center, and floor assayed $77.84 a ton. The vein on the north side of the drift at the face is half an inch to 1 inch wide and assayed $13.46 a ton. Both veins are well mineralized with arsenopyrite, and some pieces show free gold. The country rock is a hard silicified schist.

NORTH STAR

The North Star and North Star Extension claims (nos. 5 and 7, fig. 17) are in the lower part of Skoogy Gulch about a quarter of a mile north of Twin Creek. The North Star lies across the gulch and the Extension runs westward up the steep slope toward Pedro Dome. They are the property of H. F. Faulkner.

A tunnel running westward from Skoogy Gulch crosses under the highway, above which are some open cuts and a shallow shaft, now caved. These have been driven on a vein that trends N. 84° W. and dips 85° S. It is said that ore yielding $5,000 in gold was recovered from the shaft. As exposed in the tunnel (no. 7, fig. 17), this vein is from 1 inch to 4 inches wide and consists of white quartz frozen to a dark, heavily silicified schist. Some of the quartz carries a little sulphide, but in general it has no visible metallic mineralization. Of five samples taken in the 140 feet of the tunnel length the richest assayed $1.72 a ton. This vein cuts across a lenticular mass of quartz lying parallel to the schistosity, which dips 15° SE. It also cuts across a 30-inch aplite dike which strikes north and dips 15° E. and which is exposed just inside the timbers about 50 feet from the mouth of the tunnel. The vein as seen in the open cuts above the highway is from 3 to 6 inches wide and in places lies along the contact of schist and a dike of coarse porphyritic granite. About 140 feet north of this vein another 5-inch quartz vein in schist has been opened by a few pits from which, it is said, a ton of $35 ore was recovered.

A vein called by Mr. Faulkner the Big Lead is exposed along the old wagon road on the east side of Skoogy Gulch just south of his cabin. A tunnel, caved at the mouth, is 150 feet south of the cabin at the road level. This is said to be 100 feet long and to cross the south wall of the vein about 60 feet from the mouth. Another tunnel 25 feet lower and 260 feet farther south is also a crosscut. It runs due north and is said to be 200 feet long, to reach the north wall of the

Big Lead, and to be continued by a drift 17 feet in length running east along the north wall. The south wall was cut 100 feet from the portal. In this tunnel there was said to be 6 to 8 feet of soft, crushed white quartz on the south wall, which contained some gold. **Mr.** Faulkner states that some years ago an engineer, after making careful panning tests of the whole width of the lode as exposed in this tunnel, estimated that the whole ore body would average $4 a ton. This tunnel was caved in 1931 and could not be inspected. The material on the dump is all heavily iron-stained mineralized schist and quartzite similar to material along the road, a sample of which is described below. At the east end of the North Star claim, about 700 feet east of Faulkner's cabin and between the old road and new highway, there are several shallow shafts, none of which could be entered. These apparently were sunk on what seems to be the same zone as that shown along the road in the bottom of Skoogy Gulch. These shafts are so placed as to indicate a mineralized zone at least 50 feet wide. The dumps show much iron-stained crushed schist and quartz. Some boulders of heavy arsenopyrite-stibnite ore were found in one dump. Three grab samples of material, one from each of the dumps, assayed 23 cents to $3.66 a ton; the highest value was shown by the sample from the southernmost shafts.

Where this wide zone, the strike of which is essentially east, crosses the old road on the east side of Skoogy Gulch there is evidence of silicification and mineralization over a width of 75 feet 6 inches. The zone shows an alternation of schist, altered dike rocks, quartz veinlets, and faults, all of which look mineralized. Samples were cut in 17 separate sections across the lode, one of each type of material. Most of these samples contained no gold, and the highest assay from material just north of the tunnel mouth was 43 cents to the ton. The sample represented by this assay was a granular, highly altered brick-red dike rock containing irregular veinlets and bunches of manganese oxide. Mr. Faulkner states that just inside the tunnel mouth a winze was sunk on similar material that yielded some high assays in gold.

The North Star Extension claim covers part of the old Central Star (no. 8, fig. 17), which was described by Prindle,[44] who states that in 1909 the property was developed by a 65-foot shaft and 200 feet of tunnel.

A tunnel at an elevation of 1,780 feet on the south side of the west fork of Skoogy Gulch was driven west through schists for 50 feet to a dike of quartz porphyry 20 feet wide. This dike strikes N. 30° W. and dips 45° SW.

---

[44] Prindle, L. M., Auriferous quartz veins in the Fairbanks district: U.S. Geol. Survey Bull. 442, pp. 223-224, 1910.

The old Central Star shaft has been abandoned for years. The dump is composed mainly of schist but contains some fragments of quartz porphyry. There was little ore on the dump. It is reported that in 1916 some ore was milled on the ground in a home-made 1-stamp mill driven by a 6-horsepower gasoline engine.

THOMPSON & BURNS

The Thompson & Burns tunnel is just above the Central Star shaft on the south side of the west fork of Skoogy Gulch at an elevation of 2,100 feet. This tunnel, now caved about 30 feet from the mouth, with an extensive dump now overgrown with brush, was driven N. 70° W. along a fracture dipping 80° S., and the dump reveals reddish-yellow crushed brecciated schist and dike rock. Similar material was seen in place at Faulkner's Big Lead, in Skoogy Gulch, and at the head of Granite Creek, west of Pedro Dome. Of two grab samples of material of this character one assayed 83 cents to the ton and the other had no value. It is said that this work was done by the Million Dollar Corporation. Apparently no development work has been done on this property for several years.

BURNET GALENA

The old workings of the Burnet Galena claim (no. 9, fig. 17) are about 300 feet northwest of milepost 18 on the Steese Highway. The developments seen include an old shaft, an open cut, and a caved tunnel. The country rock is dark quartz diorite intruded by both coarse and fine grained granite porphyry. Both types of igneous rocks are cut by veinlets of quartz of at least two ages. No vein was seen to contain any sulphides, but on the dump there were several sacks of galena-jamesonite-cerusite ore that is said to have come from a narrow, flat-lying veinlet in the open cut.

No work has recently been done on this claim.

ZIMMERMAN

In the hydraulic cut on the Zimmerman property, on Twin Creek a quarter of a mile northeast of the mouth (no. 10, fig. 17), are extensive exposures of mineralized quartz diorite and schist. The cut had just been completed on August 25, 1931, and the final clean-up was made shortly afterward. The cut was 150 feet wide and 300 feet long. Near its southwest or lower end a fault zone that strikes east and dips 85° N. cuts the formation. The fault zone itself consists of 11 feet of blue clay gouge in which is a large amount of fragmental quartz and silicified schist. Some of the fragments contain arsenopyrite and carry the peculiar greenish-yellow stain that characterizes the richer ores of the district.

Northeast of the gouge streak the rock is quartz diorite, similar to that on Pedro Dome. For 7 feet above the fault the diorite is badly crushed, but farther to the northeast it is less altered, breaks in blocky forms, and is cut by several minor fault fractures striking from west to N. 60° W. About 55 feet north of the main fault there is a 7-foot zone of crushed diorite cut by a large number of quartz veins that strike N. 60° W. to west and form a hard rib across the cut. Northeastward from this zone the mineralization gradually died out, and unaltered diorite was seen at the north end of the bedrock cut just south of the wing dam.

Southwest of the main fault the rock is a highly silicified schist with many quartz veinlets and everywhere contains a small amount of finely disseminated arsenopyrite. The rock is bluish gray, hard, and heavier than the normal quartz-mica schist. This rock for at least 70 feet south of the main fault is much broken and crushed, and there are several well-defined slip planes striking from N. 70° W. to west and dipping north, all roughly parallel to the main fault.

In this zone 26 samples were taken, each representing a different type of material. None of the samples of the altered quartz diorite north of the fault carried either gold or silver. Even those in which quartz vein material was present showed no more than a trace of gold and silver. The silicified mineralized schist south of the fault in the main also proved to carry only a trace of precious metals, though a few samples showed as much as $1.66 a ton. This highest assay was obtained from a sample of a 3-foot zone of silicified schist that was found 60 feet south of the main fault. In that sample there was more than the average quantity of sulphide present.

BIRCH & ANDERSON

The old Birch & Anderson workings (no. 11, fig. 17) a quarter of a mile above the highway on Granite Creek, were relocated in July 1930 by Robinson & Lieman as the Hoover claim. Neither the shaft on the ridge nor the tunnel at the creek level could be entered in August 1931, as both were caved. The shaft is about 75 feet above the tunnel and was sunk at a point where some rich float was found. The dump consists of quartz-mica schist with a large amount of vein quartz, the whole having apparently come from a fractured zone that strikes east. A grab sample of this material from the dump assayed $1.23 a ton. The tunnel is driven N. 50° E. and is said to be 390 feet long and to cut the south side of a big ledge at a point 60 feet from the portal. The first ledge cut is reported to be 18 feet wide and to strike east. It is said that a little ore milled at the custom plant at Chena yielded $8 a ton, and that at one time there was a small ball mill at the mouth of the tunnel in which 5 tons of ore that averaged $8 a ton was treated. The dump of this tunnel is large. On the north side there is about 700 tons of quartzite schist with a small amount of quartz. A grab sample from various places on this part of the dump assayed 23 cents to the ton. The southern part of the dump is a bluish altered schist somewhat crushed and iron-stained and containing more quartz than the other part. A grab sample from the southern dump assayed 43 cents to the ton. Near the tunnel mouth there is about 50 tons of material that was apparently set aside as ore and that consists of quartz with some pyrite, arsenopyrite, and stibnite mixed with schist, the whole being much crushed and iron-stained. A grab sample of this material assayed 86 cents to the ton. A picked sample of quartz and sulphide ore from this pile carried $2.09 to the ton.

GILMORE AND STEAMBOAT CREEKS

Many years ago some lode claims were located and a little prospecting was done on Rose Creek, a tributary of Gilmore Creek, and on Steamboat Creek, a tributary of Pedro Creek from the north. These prospects were briefly described by Chapin,[45] but apparently they have long been abandoned.

ESTER DOME AREA

All the mines and most of the prospects on Ester Dome are southeast of the highest point of the mountain, in part because this area is more accessible but also, in a measure, because of the greater difficulty of prospecting on the streams north of the summit. Furthermore, the structure of Ester Dome seems to have restricted the area of most intense metallization to the southeast flank of the dome. This structural control is discussed more fully on pages 63–64. As shown in figure 18, the greatest amount of development is in a northward-trending zone that includes the lower parts of the ridges which extend southeast from the summit of the dome. This localization of lode deposits occurs in general near the crest of a low northward-trending anticline on the flanks of which the cleavage of the Birch Creek schist dips either east-southeast or west-northwest at relatively low angles. Lying parallel to the general structural trend are two inconspicuous outcrops of granite porphyry that are exposed along the crest of the ridge between Eva Creek and St. Patrick Creek and in the placer workings on both of these creeks.

MOTHER

The Mother group of nine claims lies on the west fork of Nugget Gulch on the northwest side of Ester Dome (no. 1, fig. 18) at an

---

[45] Chapin, Theodore, op. cit. (Bull. 592), pp. 345–346.

elevation of 1,200 feet, about 2½ miles south of the Alaska Railroad in Goldstream Valley. The property belongs to Stipp, Logan & Murphy and is sometimes called the Murphy mine. It is reached by trail, a distance of about 4 miles from the section house at mile 455 on the Alaska Railroad or 12 miles northwest of the town of Ester.

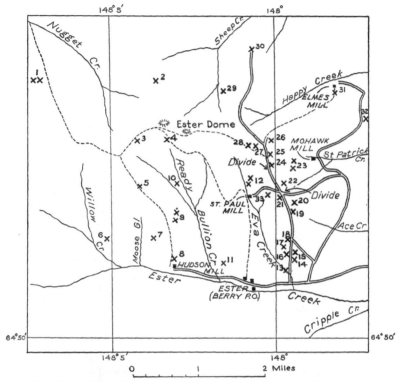

FIGURE 18.—Map of Ester Dome area, showing location of mines and prospects described in this report.

1. Mother.	13. Little Eva.	25. First Chance.
2. Grant.	14. Eva No. 2.	26. Bondholder.
3. McQueen.	15. Curlew.	27. Prometheus.
4. Farmer.	16. Blue Bird.	28. Big Blue.
5. St. Jude.	17. Combination.	29. Michley.
6. Maloney.	18. McDonald.	30. Sanford.
7. Hudson.	19, 20. Ryan.	31. Elmes.
8. Ready Bullion.	21. Fair Chance.	32. Grant.
9. Silver Dollar.	22. Billy Sunday.	33. Clipper.
10, 11. Vuyovich.	23. Mohawk.	
12. St. Paul.	24. Wandering Jew.	

Developments on this ground include several open cuts and 3 tunnels, 1 near the creek level and 2 near the crest of the ridge to the east. All these openings are caved and inaccessible, but a new cut near the upper tunnels had exposed the ledge, which is also visible at the point where the stream crosses it. There are numerous big boulders of reddish quartz breccia float all along the ledge.

The ledge strikes east and stands nearly vertical. At the creek level it is 20 feet wide and consists of brecciated iron-stained quartz and silicified schist. A sample across this width assayed 46 cents to the ton. In the cut near the top of the ridge a quarter of a mile east of the creek the ledge consists of 10 feet of quartz breccia on the north wall and 10 feet of bluish clay with quartz fragments above the south wall. The quartz next the north wall showed evidence of mineralization and is reported to average $20 a ton in a small area where the upper work was being done. The clays and quartz carry only a few cents to the ton. Some pieces of high-grade free-gold ore were seen.

The Mother ledge is large and might be of commercial value. Insufficient work had been done up to 1931 to warrant the expression of an opinion as to its probable worth, but apparently it merited further prospecting.

GRANT

On the divide between Sheep and Nugget Creeks (no. 2, fig. 18), covering ground in which a boulder of high-grade ore was discovered in the early days is a group of claims held by O. M. Grant. In the saddle about three quarters of a mile north of the monument at the summit of Ester Dome there is a shaft over 60 feet deep on a vein striking N. 10° W. and dipping 65° E. The vein had been stoped both north and south of the shaft for at least 40 feet, but as the stopes were caved and the incline coated with ice it was impossible to examine the underground conditions.

The vein has been traced both north and south for some distance by pits which indicate that it was from 5 to 6 inches wide. The quartz seen on the dump is rather white, much of it frozen to the quartzite schist walls, and contains arsenopyrite and stibnite in small amounts. A grab sample from various parts of the dump of material that appeared to be the ore assayed $9.22 to the ton.

It is said that about 10 tons of ore was taken out from this mine a few years ago.

FARMER

The workings of the Farmer lode (no. 4, fig. 18) are near the head of the west fork of Ready Bullion Creek at an elevation of 1,925 feet. The main tunnel is caved at the mouth. There is no mining equipment on the ground, and the ore bins are in bad repair. The road leading to the lower tunnel and camp is overgrown with brush.

About 20 feet above the mouth of the lower tunnel the top of an old stope is visible, but its condition was unsafe. The vein is fairly well exposed in a pillar. It strikes N. 25° E. and dips 52° W. The hanging wall is a quartz-mica schist lying horizontal. Immediately below the hanging-wall selvage there is 4 inches of iron-stained quartz followed by 14 inches of crushed bluish schist, and this by 2 feet of iron-stained fault breccia made up of fragments of schist and quartz lying above the footwall.

A sample taken across 4 feet of ledge matter in the pillar assayed $7.06 to the ton. No maps of the workings could be found, and the extent of the ore shoot is not known. It is reported that good ore from the Farmer vein was milled at the St. Paul mill on Eva Creek some years ago.

ST. JUDE

The St. Jude No. 1 and No. 2 claims (no. 5, fig. 18), held since September 1930 by Mrs. Bertha Olsen, are on the ridge west of Ready Bullion Creek at an elevation of 2,000 feet. There are two old shafts on this property, now caved, which indicate that the vein strikes N. 35° W. and dips northwest at a rather flat angle, possibly 30°. One dump, from a shaft which from the amount of material excavated is probably more than 75 feet deep, consists of rather dark mica schist, with very little quartz. A few pieces of quartz show the usual sulphides.

MALONEY

William Maloney has a claim a short distance north of Ester Creek (no. 6, fig. 18) at an elevation of 1,300 feet on the point of the hill east of Willow Creek. A 90-foot shaft had been sunk on this property, but in 1931 it could not be entered. It is said to intersect the ledge at a depth of 50 feet. The ledge is said to be from 12 to 14 feet wide, to strike east-northeast, and to dip southeast. The dump of the shaft is mainly quartzite schist, and the ore pile is largely a blue clay gouge with some quartz carrying arsenopyrite and stibnite.

READY BULLION

The Ready Bullion group of 18 claims, comprising the Geneva, Mary Stay, Hosanna, Hudson (no. 7, fig. 18), Horseshoe, Ready Bullion (no. 8, fig. 18), Lode Fraction, Stibnite No. 1, Stibnite No. 2, Borovich, Borovich Fraction, Borovich No. 2, Native Daughter, South Pole, North Pole, Camp, Sunflower, and Fraction, covers 5,000 feet of a vein system that lies north of Ester Creek near the crest of the ridge between Ready Bullion and Moose Creeks. This ground is the property of the Eva Quartz Mining Co. and includes a mine referred to in earlier reports [46] as the Hudson mine. The old Hudson mill is on this ground, near Ester Creek about 1½ miles west of Berry post office, at the old town of Ester, and the Hudson shaft is near the northwest corner of the group. The claims trend

---

[46] Smith, P. S., op. cit. (Bull. 525), pp. 203-206. Chapin, Theodore, op. cit. (Bull. 592), pp. 350-352.

in a north-northeast direction and extend nearly to the Markich ground, at the forks of Ready Bullion Creek.

This group, in part relocations of abandoned ground, was assembled by G. B. Stevens and Nick Borovich in 1926 as the Eva Quartz Mining Co. and has produced every year since. Most of the production has come from high-grade ore taken out during the development of a wide zone of low-grade material. The ore was treated in a mill on the property a short distance south of the mouth of the lower tunnel. This mill has a rail grizzly set to 1½-inch size, a 7 by 9 inch Blake crusher set to one half inch, a Challenge feeder, and two Nissen stamps. The mill and pumps are operated by a 25-horsepower steam engine supplied by a 50-horsepower coal-burning boiler. A well, sunk in the mill building, assures adequate water supply for winter use.

The main development consists of two drift tunnels, one at an elevation of 1,000 feet on the Borovich claim and the other at 1,100 feet on the Hosanna claim. A large amount of prospecting that has been done on the surface to the north indicates that the zone of mineralization extends for the full length of the group and probably beyond it into the adjoining ground on the north. That there are several veins is also evident from the surface work, though the main underground development is for the most part along one zone. In September 1931 the owners had just found the outcrop of a new vein lying east of those formerly worked, in which there was some high-grade ore.

The upper tunnel was caved at the mouth and could not be examined. The underground plans (see pl. 8) show that it is approximately 600 feet long with 6 crosscuts aggregating 240 feet and varying from 20 to 100 feet in length. Much of the work in the upper tunnel is shown by plate 8 to be in the ore zone.

The mouth of the lower tunnel, the main working adit, is 570 feet south of the upper tunnel and 100 feet lower. There is an ore bin with a capacity of about 25 tons at the end of the dump, and a small blacksmith shop and change house near the entrance. The tunnel is equipped with 8-pound rails throughout its length of 1,280 feet. The ground, particularly in the ore zone near the face, is very heavy and requires stronger timbers than were originally placed, so the last 100 feet of the tunnel was caved and could not be examined. The crosscuts in the ore zone were likewise caved, but one, no. 3, was reopened so that samples could be cut for assay. This tunnel attains a maximum depth of 160 feet below the surface.

As shown by the cross section (pl. 8) a fairly large stope has been mined between the lower and upper tunnels, but in June 1931 none of this work was accessible. This stope was about 160 feet long and about 40 feet high on a vein about 8 feet wide and is reported to have yielded about 3,600 tons of ore which averaged $6.09 to the ton, or a total value of $21,900. Near the face of the upper tunnel a small stope yielded a few hundred tons of $11.84 ore from a vein averaging 3 feet wide. Some ore was also taken from a stope in the first drift in the lower tunnel. Apparently this stope was about 60 feet long and from 2 to 10 feet wide, though most of the ore taken out came from a 2 to 3 foot band of higher-grade ore near the east or hanging-wall side of the vein. This stope was badly caved and could not be examined in detail. The lower tunnel for the first 200 feet runs through medium-dark mica schists that lie nearly horizontal or have a slight dip to the east-southeast. About 225 feet from the mouth the tunnel is crossed by a fault striking N. 50° E. and dipping 78° S. Movement along this fault was normal, as is shown by the small displacement of some quartz veinlets on the west side of the drift. The drift, 450 feet in from the mouth of the tunnel and on the main Ready Bullion vein, runs north for 100 feet but is badly caved about 60 feet from the tunnel. There are several raises, and the area above had been stoped but was all caved in June 1931, so that only two pillars of the ore just above the level were visible. These were on the hanging-wall or east side of the nearly vertical vein and were 4 feet wide. Samples cut across these pillars assayed 43 cents and $6.06 to the ton. The vein is crushed and has slickensided surfaces on the hanging wall and at several different places within a width of 4 feet. It is said that in places in the stope above the drift the vein was 10 feet or more wide.

Beyond the first drift the main adit runs N. 10° W. for about 100 feet through practically horizontal quartz-mica schists cut in several places by veinlets of quartz, some of which show a little mineralization. It was stated by the owners that this zone was all ore. Careful sampling in six cuts, each representing a length of 20 feet, showed a range of values from 23 cents to $1.26 a ton, the average for the entire width being 43 cents. The eastern boundary of this zone is a 10-inch vein of hard, solid white quartz that averages $20 a ton. This vein strikes N. 48° W. and dips 75° NE. About 80 feet to the north it merges with the main vein just beyond the A raise. The small vein in this raise is 6 inches wide, and a carefully cut sample assayed $11.66 a ton over the entire width. About 100 feet north of the A raise the main vein is cut off by a fault that strikes N. 58° E. and dips 50° S. Movement on this plane was normal, and the throw was about 40 feet. The segment of the vein north of the fault is shown in raise 6. (See plan, pl. 8.) This raise goes through to the surface but was caved about 30 feet above the tunnel level. It is stated that 60 feet up in this raise a crosscut was run to the west through mineralized schist for a distance of 51 feet. Assays made for the operations indicate that the first 20 feet of material west of the hanging-wall slip can be considered ore but that the remainder of the drift would not repay the cost of mining and milling, though it is mineralized. One sample taken across 4 feet of the hanging-wall side of the vein as exposed 30 feet up the raise in a pillar just below the cave assayed $6.86 to the ton. The vein here strikes N. 15° E. and dips 70° E. There is 12 inches of gouge on the hanging wall, between which and another slip plane there is 36 inches of crushed schist and quartz mixed with clay.

Beyond raise 6 the main adit turns northwest, cutting through a broad fault zone with three well-marked fault planes that strike N. 53° E. The southern fault plane dips 70° N., the central plane dips 70° S., and the northern plane dips 45° S. The main vein was displaced approximately 130 feet by this zone, the segment beyond the fault zone being found to the west as the result of normal faulting. The southern fault is marked by a zone 6 feet wide that includes a mixture of crushed schist, fragments of quartz as large as 4 inches, and clay. The central fault zone is 4 feet wide and contains much the same assortment of material as the south fault. The north fault shown in the adit is not shown in the drift south of the audit near raise 1, and movement along the main vein was evidently later than this fault.

The drift south from the main adit near raise 1 was evidently driven under the impression that the main vein was shifted to the west—south of the fault—whereas the development shows the contrary to be the fact. At any rate, ore in blocks as much as 4 feet in diameter assaying $1.23 a ton was found in the drift on the south fault, and at the face of the crosscut south of the south fault a vein was cut that strikes north and dips 80° W. This vein, which is different from that shown in the main adit, is 5½ feet wide, with badly crushed quartz lying between 1 foot of gouge on the hanging wall and 2 inches of gouge on the footwall. A sample across the full width assayed 43 cents to the ton.

The adit north of raise 1 follows the main vein, which here trends a little more west of north than usual. The country rock east of the vein is a hard, dense quartzite; the rock to the west is micaceous schist. This part of the ore body, which is directly under the ore shown in the upper tunnel, had been opened extensively and sampled by at least three engineers. It was caved in June 1931 and could not be examined. The ore between the upper and lower tunnels was said to have a width of 7.9 feet and to assay $6.09 a ton. The no. 3

crosscut was reopened for sampling and was found to contain a zone at least 21 feet wide of crushed schist and quartz which carries more than $1.23 a ton in gold. The gold is concentrated chiefly in the first 10 feet below the hanging wall, which gave average assays of $13.39 a ton.

The Ready Bullion main vein has been opened and reopened by geologic processes several times, with deposition of several varieties of quartz. The latest metallization brought in arsenopyrite and some stibnite accompanied by free gold. There is also in the rich ore a fibrous mineral that appears to be an antimony-lead sulphide, differing from stibnite in its reactions with etching media. This may be bournonite or boulangerite. Some very high grade ore of this character was seen on the dump. Postmineral movement has been intense along the main vein, and as a consequence there are heavy clay gouges on the walls and in various places in the ore. Oxidation has penetrated to the greatest depth obtained in the workings (160 feet), and iron, manganese, arsenic, and antimony oxidation products are present everywhere. There is, however, much unaltered primary sulphide ore even in ore from the upper tunnel.

There are practically no reserves of ore actually blocked out in the Ready Bullion workings. There is, however, every indication of the presence of at least one wide mineralized zone which has minable ore on the hanging-wall side over widths of 6 to 10 feet. There are also several smaller veins exposed, any one of which may contain minable ore bodies. The faulting problem is not serious, and the movement on all the faults exposed is normal. The mining problem is one of heavy ground, which has been met in many places by the use of properly set heavy timber and presents no insuperable obstacle.

SILVER DOLLAR

The Silver Dollar group of claims (no. 9, fig. 18) is on the west side of Ready Bullion Creek about 1½ miles north of Ester Creek. This group has produced in the past about $4,000, taken from a shaft and tunnel at an elevation of about 1,300 feet, 150 feet above the stream level. The property belongs to Dan Makaich but in 1931 was under lease to Dan Radovich, who had shipped some ore in 1930.

The vein strikes N. 30° E. and dips 68° SE. Southwest of the upper tunnel there are several shallow shafts, which were caved in June 1931. The upper tunnel was caved a short distance in from the mouth, but a 30-foot winze at the mouth was open. At the bottom of the winze the vein is 5 feet wide between definite walls and consists largely of quartz but contains some altered schist. All the material between the walls was badly crushed by postmineral faulting. A sample across the entire width of the vein assayed $9.63

to the ton. There was about 10 tons of ore on the dump, a grab sample of which assayed $74.76 to the ton.

A tunnel started from a point near the creek level had been driven 515 feet in a general S. 65° W. direction through schists dipping 15° SSE. The tunnel was apparently north of the vein, and if this conclusion is correct a crosscut to the south near the face will be necessary to intersect the Silver Dollar vein.

VUYOVICH

On the east side of Ready Bullion Creek at an elevation of 1,250 feet John Vuyovich has a prospect (no. 10, fig. 18) on a narrow vein that strikes about N. 50° E. The tunnel is caved at the mouth, but from the size of the dump it must be from 50 to 60 feet long. This vein, which has a maximum width of 6 inches, is said to have yielded some very rich ore. Ore on the dump appears to be the usual iron-stained, crushed quartz, some of which shows free gold, and panning tests indicate considerable arsenopyrite and free gold throughout most of it. The country rock at the tunnel is a dark micaceous schist, but in some prospect pits on the vein farther up the hill to the northeast the rock is a quartz-mica schist.

Mr. Vuyovich also holds the claim on which his cabin stands (no. 11, fig. 18) on the east side of Ready Bullion Creek about a quarter of a mile north of Ester Creek. A tunnel running N. 20° E. has been driven about 100 feet along a crushed iron-stained zone of schist in which there are a number of quartz veinlets. This zone dips 85° E. Most of the tunnel is tightly lagged, but at the face the zone is 4 feet wide. Some of the quartz carries lenses of arsenopyrite and of stibnite or a mixture of the two sulphides. The material in the face is oxidized and pans free gold as well as sulphides.

About 100 feet south of the tunnel an open cut in the low cliff along the creek exposes a 10-foot face of altered schist with a 2 to 4 inch stringer of mineralized quartz lying parallel to the schistosity, which here strikes N. 20° E. and dips 4° E.

ST. PAUL

The St. Paul property (no. 12, fig. 18), on the west fork of Eva Creek, extends from the mill at an elevation of 1,150 feet northeast-ward to an upper tunnel and surface workings at an elevation of 1,500 feet. It is the property of McCann, Thomas, Mickley, and the Hagel estate. The mill on Eva Creek is operated by a steam engine supplied by a wood-burning 20-horsepower boiler, and is equipped with a 7 by 9 inch crusher of the Blake type, a Challenge feeder, and a 7-foot Lane mill of the Chile type. Water is supplied from springs above the mill. The mill at times treats the ore for other producers, and when so operating a charge of $5 a ton is made for milling.

About 10 tons ground to 20 mesh for each shift of 10 hours is said to be the usual output of the mill.

The tunnel near the mill, driven in a north-northeast direction, is said to be 300 feet long but has been abandoned and allowed to cave. The dump is entirely quartz-mica schist. The upper tunnel now caved at the mouth is at an elevation of 1,475 feet about a quarter of a mile north-northeast of the mill. Caved stopes on the hillside above it indicate that it follows the vein in a N. 30° E. direction. Mr. McCann reports that the tunnel was driven 250 feet on the vein which ranged from 3 to 4 feet in width, with a 6 to 8 inch streak of quartz next the hanging wall. The vein above the tunnel has a dip of 45° W., but it steepens to 70° in a winze below the tunnel. All the ore above the tunnel level for its full length had been stoped, this stope having yielded about 1,000 tons of $30 ore, which was hauled to the St. Paul mill. The vein was not faulted above the tunnel level, but in the winze, 60 to 70 feet below, there is a flat fault. ·

The dump of the upper tunnel is composed largely of iron-stained biotite schist, with a considerable amount of clay gouge and quartz. A grab sample of the crushed material on this dump that presumably came from the vein assayed 72 cents to the ton, and there were also on it some large pieces of heavy stibnite-arsenopyrite-quartz ore and a few pieces of high-grade gold quartz.

STAY

The Stay property, which covers about 115 acres, consists of six claims—the Little Eva (no. 13, fig. 18), Eva No. 2 (no. 14), Curlew No. 1 (no. 15), Curlew No. 2, Rose, and Comet—lying north of Ester Creek on the point of the ridge east of Eva Creek and about half a mile east of Berry post office. There is no machinery on this property, and all work has been done by hand. A small blacksmith shop is located at the mouth of the Little Eva adit, near Eva Creek about a quarter of a mile north of the road in Ester Creek, at an elevation of 740 feet. The ore produced at several places on this property in past years has been milled at the Ready Bullion mill, 3 miles west of the mine; the Mohawk mill, 2 miles north; or the St. Paul mill, 2½ miles by road north-northwest.

During 1930 and 1931 there was produced from the adit tunnel and the Stay shafts, on the crest of the ridge, about 700 tons of ore which yielded about $16,000. Most of this ore came from the adit, and it yielded a little more than 1 ounce of gold to the ton. A little ore recovered during sinking and drifting in several shafts at the north end of the Little Eva and Eva No. 2 claims carried as much as $60 to $70 a ton. In 1931 there were 4 men working on the property in two localities.

Most of the development work has been done in the Little Eva adit near the mouth of Eva Creek. (See fig. 19.) This adit was about 570 feet long in June 1931. It follows a badly faulted vein. which in general is from 6 to 18 inches in width, stands nearly vertical, and strikes N. 27° W. There are six faults, each of which has displaced the vein from 6 to 40 feet and along each of which the movement has been normal. The faults strike N. 10°–51° E., their average direction being about northeast and their dips to the north or northwest at

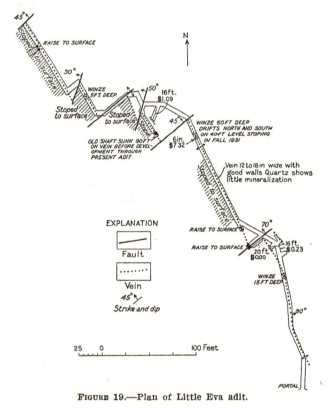

FIGURE 19.—Plan of Little Eva adit.

angles of 30° to 70°, the average dip being about 45°. As a result of this faulting the vein is continually offset to the west. This has brought the vein at the inner face of the adit continually nearer to the surface, and it is probable that the segment of vein beyond the fault in the face of the tunnel will be found near the level of the creek.

Practically all the ore above the adit level which by panning test was judged to contain an ounce or more of gold to the ton has been stoped and milled. Below the tunnel the vein is developed by several winzes. The first winze, at a point 120 feet from the portal of the adit, is 15 feet deep and shows the vein to be 8 to 11 inches wide;

the second winze, at about 300 feet from the portal, is 60 feet deep, with drifts to both north and south on the 40-foot level. This winze had no ladders and so could not be inspected in June 1931. The third winze is 5 feet deep and is about 70 feet from the face. These workings indicate that the vein and its metal content persist in depth, and it seems reasonable to assume that for the entire length of the tunnel, 570 feet, the vein will be continuous for a depth of at least 50 feet and have an average width of at least 8 inches. These figures indicate a probable total of 1,350 tons of ore, which, on the basis of the ore already mined, should yield at least $15 a ton at the mill, or a total of about $20,000. On a narrow vein of this sort considerable wall rock must also be taken out to afford working room, and this would add to the cost of mining or dilute the value of the material that is handled.

In some places the schist wall rock east of the main vein (there are no crosscuts west of the vein) is cut by numerous stringers of quartz that follow the planes of schistosity, which are here nearly horizontal. This schist contains from 23 cents to as much as $1 a ton, as shown by two samples cut across a width of 16 and 20 feet. Obviously, rock of so low a tenor cannot be profitably mined, but it is not at all improbable that in places the schist may be sufficiently mineralized to be minable, and all such material should be sampled during development operations.

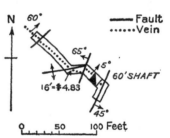

FIGURE 20.—Plan of 40-foot level, Eva No. 2 shaft, Stay property.

Considerable work has been done on the Stay property near the northwest corner of the Little Eva claim and the northwestern part of the Eva No. 2 claim near the road to the Mohawk mill. Several shallow shafts from 12 to 60 feet deep are scattered over an area about 200 feet square. In all these shafts veins are exposed, and some high-grade ore has been taken from them.

The Eva No. 2 shaft is 60 feet deep, with about 40 feet of drifts on the 40-foot level. (See fig. 20.) The shaft was sunk on a short segment of the vein lying between two parallel faults. Movement along the faults was normal and the throw was small. The southern fault has 3 feet of crushed schist, ore, and clay between heavily slickensided walls. The fault just north of the shaft has only 2 inches of gouge, and the fault at the north end of the northwest drift has 8 inches of crushed schist. The vein is from 4 to 6 inches wide and strikes N. 50° W. It carries high-grade ore, and the schist on both sides is mineralized. Ore taken out in sinking the shaft is reported to have milled $40 a ton, and all the material that came from the shaft and drifts carried $3 or more in gold to the ton. Samples taken on both sides of the east-west part of the drift just north of the shaft assayed $4.83 a ton over a width of 16 feet. The samples were cut in two channels, one on each side of the drift. A grab sample of the waste dump gave an assay of 43 cents to the ton.

A caved shaft 60 feet southwest of the one described above could not be entered, but the dump shows considerable mineralized schist. A grab sample of the entire dump yielded on assay $1.23 to the ton.

Three shallow shafts about 60 feet apart on the west side of the road northwest of the 60-foot shaft first described are connected 20 feet below the surface by drifts. Most of the work is badly caved, so that the material they traversed was not sampled. A strong vein in these holes is apparently a continuation of the vein in the 60-foot shaft.

In the fall of 1931 a new shaft about 100 feet south of the 60-foot shaft had been sunk by Mr. Stay on a vein 36 inches wide that strikes N. 65° W. and dips 50° NE. The gold is concentrated in an 18-inch streak on the hanging wall that assays $1.92 to the ton and an 18-inch streak on the footwall that assays $55.38 to the ton. A 12-inch horse of sericitized schist between these streaks carries only 26 cents to the ton.

In an area on the north end of the Eva No. 2 and Little Eva claims there is a mineralized zone striking northwest that, as shown by developments in August 1931, is at least 70 feet wide and over 200 feet long. This zone contains some rich veins, and all the wall rock seems to be mineralized. Whether or not it will be possible to work this body as a whole remains to be determined by more systematic development and sampling.

On the Curlew (Old Granite) claim, at the north end of Mr. Stay's property, about a mile up the ridge road to the north from the Little Eva adit, there are several shafts on both sides of the road, which after penetrating 10 to 20 feet of silt go into a body of quartz porphyry that is much altered and mineralized. This is the largest body of granitic rock known on Ester Dome. It appears to be at least a quarter of a mile long and to have a maximum width on the Curlew ground of about 300 feet. Most of the shafts were so badly caved that they could not be entered. One shaft east of the road is open for a depth of 40 feet and has a crosscut at the bottom. At the bottom of the shaft and for 15 feet east of it is a zone of shattered, iron-stained soft altered quartz porphyry, cut by innumerable quartz stringers, which in general strike N. 50° W. and dip 50° NE. A sample cut across this material assayed 23 cents to the ton. The last 15 feet of this crosscut and the face is in white sericitized and kaolinized quartz porphyry that does not appear to be mineralized.

M'DONALD

J. H. McDonald and Lewis Morton held a group of four claims, north of the Little Eva group, on the ridge between Eva and Ester Creeks, about 1 mile northeast of the town of Ester. This group includes the Blue Bird, Blue Bird Fraction, Combination, and Mc-Donald claims. There is no mechanical equipment on the property, all work having been done by hand.

The Blue Bird shaft (no. 16, fig. 18) is near the east center of the claim, at the side of the road from Ester to the Mohawk mill. In 1931 it was being worked under lease by J. Y. Bigelow, who had already milled 240 tons of $19 ore when the writer visited the property on June 13. The shaft is an inclined shaft 80 feet deep on a vein that strikes N. 35° W. and dips 65° NE. (See fig. 21.) On the 20-foot level there is a drift 10 feet long to the south which shows the vein 8 to 12 inches wide except at the face, where it had pinched to a mere fracture. On the 50-foot level the vein north of the shaft was stoped from 2 to 4 feet wide between good walls. It is said that there were streaks of high-grade ore on both footwall and hanging wall. At the north end of the drift the vein is cut off by a fault striking east that dips 50° S. The segment beyond the fault has not been found. The fault zone consists of 2 feet of crushed schist and clay. The same fault is seen at the north end of the 80-foot level about 30 feet north of the shaft. On the 80-foot level the vein was displaced about 4 feet by a small fault which cuts across the bottom of the shaft. This fault was not seen on the 50-foot level. On the 80-foot level the vein north of this fault was 6 to 8 inches wide near the fault, but about 10 feet farther north it was joined by a split from the west, north of which there was 2 feet of crushed quartz ore of good grade. In the south drift on the 80-foot level the vein consisted of rather white, little mineralized quartz and was only 3 inches wide.

A general sample of the vein taken from several pillars on the 50 and 80 foot levels assayed $14.92 a ton over a width of 12 inches. All the ground between the shaft and the north fault had been stoped to the 80-foot level, so there are no reserves of blocked-out ore. A grab sample of the ore pile on the surface assayed only $2.43 a ton, though there was some high-grade ore with visible gold in this pile.

The Combination shaft (no. 17, fig. 18) is on the top of the cliffs overlooking the Eva Creek, about an eighth of a mile west of the Ester-Mohawk road. All equipment had been removed, and the shaft was caved at the collar and could not be examined. It is said to be 100 feet deep on the incline and to follow down on a vein that strikes N. 20° W. and dips 45° E. The dump consists mainly of altered bleached quartzite schist, but some large boulders of arsenopyrite-stibnite ore are scattered over it. The vein is reported to average 3 feet in width and to carry heavy sulphide ore averaging $25 to $40 to the ton.

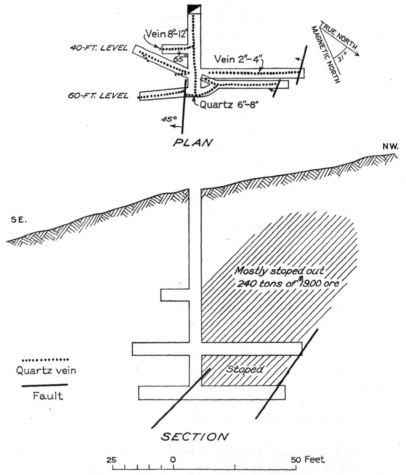

FIGURE 21.—Plan and longitudinal section, Blue Bird shaft.

Just north of McDonald's cabin on the McDonald claim (no. 18, fig. 18) there are several shafts on what appear to be four nearly parallel veins. One of these veins is on the contact between quartz porphyry and a lime silicate phase of the Birch Creek schist. Another vein farther northwest cuts biotite-quartz schists. All these veins strike about N. 40° E. and seem to stand nearly vertical. One shaft, said to be 50 feet deep, has caved and was partly filled with water.

so that it could not be examined. The remaining development work on this claim includes open cuts and pits that expose only the tops of the. veins, which are from 8 to 12 inches wide and consist of the usual quartz-arsenopyrite-stibnite ore of the district. No samples were taken for assay, but panning tests at several places indicate that the area is well worth further prospecting.

RYAN

The Ryan lode group (nos. 19, 20, fig. 18) of 7¼ patented claims lies on the ridge between Eva and St. Patrick Creeks on the southeast side of Ester Dome; the center of the group is on a low hill at an elevation of 1,275 feet. The claims were patented under mineral surveys 826, dated November 4, 1914; 1602 and 1603, dated January 1928. The Ijim, Eva, Edna, Montie, Ryan No. 1, Ryan No. 2, and Excelsior are full claims, the Gem is one quarter the size of the usual claim. The group is about 5,000 feet in length along the strike of the lode (N. 24° E.) and from 600 to 1,800 feet wide. The ownership is widely scattered, there being 64 different undivided lots, but control seems to rest with a relatively small group of persons in Fairbanks, who are represented by the First National Bank and A. W. Conradt.

So far as could be learned no ore has been shipped or milled from the Ryan lode. It has been opened by a number of pits and shallow shafts, and during one period when it was under option a tunnel 300 feet long and shaft 200 feet deep were sunk near the north center of the group. (See pl. 9.) There is no mining equipment on the ground, and much of the surface work is caved. Some of the shafts have been kept open, but in many of them the timbering is in poor condition, and unless it is replaced all the underground work will soon become inaccessible.

As a result of the study and sampling at various places on the Ryan lode it is apparent that this lode is in reality a fault zone that strikes in general about N. 20°–25° E. and dips 45°–70° E. with an average dip of 50°. The enclosing schists lie nearly horizontal or dip 10°–15° ESE. except near the hanging wall fault, where the schistosity is essentially parallel to the fault. This zone of crushed schist and quartz veins is from 40 to 70 feet wide. Apparently there is a fairly persistent zone of quartz near the hanging-wall side of the lode, as shown in shafts A and B (see pl. 9) and as is reported to have occurred in the north shaft, which is now inaccessible. This zone is from 9 to 20 feet in width and carries most of the metal content of the whole lode. Much of the movement in this zone was postmineral, for nowhere were any unbroken portions of veins seen in the underground exposures. The movement consisted largely of horizontal or strike faults rather than of dip faults. There are many planes of movement throughout the width of the zone, and the crushing of the schists has resulted in the formation of a very large amount of clay. As is well illustrated in shaft D at the south end of the ground, this mixture of crushed schist, quartz, and clay flows like mud when it is under water. All the other workings that could be entered were relatively dry, though on the 100-foot level of the main shaft the ground was sufficiently wet to be very sticky.

The northern shaft on the lode, at an elevation of 1,000 feet, is near the north center of the Ryan No. 1 claim. It was iced up and could not be examined, but the size of the dump indicated that the shaft was rather deep, and according to local reports, it had a depth of 60 feet. The material on the dump is a dark crushed schist, with much gouge and some vein quartz. One large fragment of quartz-arsenopyrite-stibnite ore was seen.

The main tunnel, at an elevation of 1,150 feet, below the road at the south end of the Ryan No. 1 claim, was caved at the mouth. The dump is extensive, and the tunnel is reported to be about 300 feet long, with three crosscuts at 50-foot intervals at the south end. Most of the dump is composed of the red schist. At the south end of the dump there is a bluish crushed schist mixed with clay and some quartz. A grab sample of this material assayed $2.15 a ton. Near the mouth of the tunnel the dump consists of red crushed schist and clay which assayed 83 cents a ton. On the southwest side of the dump there is a white sericitic schist with quartz that assayed only 23 cents a ton. A few boulders of crushed quartz-sulphide ore were seen, one of which showed free gold.

The collar of the main shaft (A) at the road, in the southwest corner of the Ryan No. 1 claim, is 30 feet above the floor of the tunnel with which it is connected. The shaft is vertical for a depth of 100 feet, and at its bottom there is a crosscut 63 feet long to the east and one 24 feet long to the west. Below the 100-foot level the shaft is said to continue vertical for about 20 feet and then to cut through the footwall of the lode, which it follows down to the 200-foot level. The air in the 100-foot level was bad in June 1931, so that only after several attempts to enter it could samples be obtained. The results of the sampling are shown on plate 9. The whole 87 feet of the east and west crosscuts is mineralized. The lode consists of a crushed zone of schist and vein quartz with a very large proportion of clay. Near the hanging wall there is more quartz than in the remainder of the zone. The average value of the whole crosscut is $4.18 a ton, but the 18 feet just under the hanging wall averages $17.13 a ton. The hanging wall is marked by about 2 feet of sticky clay gouge, marking a fault zone the movement along which has been nearly horizontal. The schists in the hanging wall lie parallel to the strike and dip of this fault. However, a short distance east, as shown on the surface, the schists dip about 15°SE. There are many other fault planes evident in the crosscut, and the footwall of the zone is probably a heavy wet gouge, as it is heavily timbered and lagged.

Near the northeast corner of the Eva claim, and on the line between that claim and the Montie, there is a 30-foot shaft (B), which shows the hanging-wall portion of the lode. The timbering at the bottom of this shaft is gone and the ladders are in bad repair. A grab sample of the material on the dump of this shaft assayed $3.64 to the ton. The average assay from two samples cut in the 10-foot drift to the east of the shaft at the 30-foot level was $3.42 a ton. The assay values of the individual samples are shown on plate 9. A 4-foot belt of badly crushed quartz, schist, and clay that lies next the hanging-wall fault assayed $7.30 a ton. The hanging-wall schist is a red mica-quartz variety that along the fault strikes N. 44° E. and dips 64° E. parallel to the lode. On the surface at a point 25 feet east of the shaft the same schists are seen to dip 15° SE. The shaft is in a zone of strong crushing, all the schist being ground to a gray clay which contains some remnants of quartz.

Near the south center of the east side line of the Eva claim, just above the road from McGlone's cabin to Ester, there is a 50-foot shaft (C) from which a crosscut to the northwest on the 50-foot level cuts across the Ryan lode. This shaft is about 100 feet north of corner 3 of the Montie claim. A grab sample from the outer edge of the dump, which consists of a reddish quartz-mica-schist containing considerable clay and crushed vein quartz, assayed $1.26 a ton. A grab sample from a smaller dump close to the collar of the shaft assayed 46 cents a ton. The assays of samples taken in the crosscut are shown in detail on plate 9. The whole crosscut from the bottom of the shaft to the face is 48 feet long. A sample taken from the entire length gives an average assay return of $3.15 a ton. There is a belt 20 feet wide just west of the shaft which averages $5.88 a ton. This material is a red crushed schist containing stringers of quartz that extend in all directions but are mostly parallel to the major structure, which strikes N. 15° E. and dips 50° ESE.

The underground work on the southern portion of the Ryan lode is at shaft D, about 120 feet west of corner 3 of the Montie claim and near the southeast corner of the Eva claim. This shaft is 65 feet deep. It was under water when visited in June 1931 but was later unwatered by the Fairbanks Exploration Co., and in July it was possible to cut samples in the crosscut on the 65-foot level. The detailed results of this sampling are shown on plate 9. A sample taken across the entire 42-foot width of the Ryan lode at this place assayed 16 cents to the ton. One quartz vein just northwest of the shaft assayed $2.06 to the ton over a width of 1½ feet. The foot-wall schist is quartzitic, and the fault plane along the footwall dips 70° E. The hanging wall is black mica schist, separated from the Ryan lode proper by a 2-foot belt of black gouge.

There are several shallow pits and a shaft, now caved, at the north end of the Ijim claim (see pl. 9), evidently sunk through rather deep overburden to locate the southward continuation of the Ryan lode. An assay of a grab sample of the dump at an old shallow shaft at this place showed no value.

A parallel vein about 250 feet west of the Ryan lode is exposed in several shafts near the north center of the Eva claim and the east center of the Edna claim. None of these workings were accessible in 1931. Some high-grade ore was noted on the dumps near the north end of the Eva claim, but a general grab sample of the dump assayed only 23 cents a ton.

The samples taken indicate that in two blocks of ground, one between shafts C and D and the other between shafts B and A, there is a total of at least 287,000 tons of material within 100 feet of the surface that contains $777,000 in gold and silver. In the north body alone the zone of richer ore near the hanging wall, which averages 14 feet in width, contains 60,000 tons of ore, having a value of $648,000, within 100 feet of the surface. Facts are not available on which to base an accurate estimate of content of the lode from shaft D at the south end to the north shaft, a total distance of 2,500 feet. If it is assumed that the ore has an average width of 37 feet, as is indicated by the samples, and a depth of 200 feet below the crest of the hill, this area contains 1,300,000 tons, which at $3.27 a ton, would have a total value of $4,157,000.

There is, however, serious doubt as to whether material carrying even as much as $5 a ton in gold can be considered ore under the mining conditions that will be met on the Ryan lode, for the ground is extremely heavy and the wall rock weak. Surface stripping also appears impracticable for a lode that dips at an angle of 45° to 50°. There is, however, the possibility that the higher-grade hanging-wall material, in a zone from 9 to 20 feet wide, that is exposed in shafts A and B, might be mined by the use of square-set timbering if the working shaft and main gangways were kept in the wall rock and workings could be maintained in the fault zone. The chief difficulty in milling the material would be in handling the slimes, for most of the material is already crushed and the particles of quartz are fractured and should grind easily.

FAIR CHANCE

The Fair Chance group (no. 21, fig. 18) is in the saddle near Mc-Glone's cabin. In addition to the Fair Chance, the Star Crystal and Frisco Fraction claims also belong to the McGlone estate. All three of the shafts in the saddle were caved in June and July 1931. The three shafts are about 50 feet apart and were worked during the winter of 1930, when about 40 tons of ore was taken out. This ore was milled during the summer of 1931, with rather disappointing results. A grab sample of this ore, which is a crushed mixture of gouge, schist, and quartz somewhat resembling the ore from the Ryan lode, assayed $5.95 a ton. It is said that the shafts, the deepest of which is 75 feet deep, show a mineralized zone that strikes N. 20° E. and dips 60° W. All the schist in this zone is more or less crushed and is said to contain several veins of quartz ore from which a total of $1,800 in gold has been recovered.

A short distance down the slope to the south-southwest of the McGlone divide there is a new crosscut tunnel on a claim owned jointly by Mrs. Miller and Jack O'Conner, of Fairbanks. In July 1931 this tunnel had a length of about 40 feet and had just penetrated to the schist bedrock in the face. The tunnel is projected to open a vein that was prospected by open cuts on the surface about 100 feet N. 40° E. from the tunnel mouth and 75 feet higher. The old dumps here are presumably material taken from the same zone of fracturing and mineralization as those exposed in the workings on the Fair Chance claim. This claim is called the Blue Bird, but it should not be confused with the Blue Bird belonging to J. H. McDonald, farther southeast on the same ridge.

BILLY SUNDAY

The Billy Sunday mine (no. 22, fig. 18) lies at the head of the south fork of St. Patrick Creek, on the southeast side of Ester Dome, at an elevation of 1,260 feet. The shaft is about one eighth of a mile northwest of the McGlone cabin, on the divide between St. Patrick and Eva Creeks. This is a patented fractional claim surveyed in 1919 under mineral survey 844 and contains about 7⅓ acres. It is the property of Smith Bros., of Fairbanks, and is in charge of E. A. Smith.

Approximately $50,000 has been produced from about 1,900 tons of ore from the Billy Sunday vein, the ore averaging over $26 a ton. This ore came principally from stopes above the 120-foot level, but a lesser amount was taken from a winze on the 200-foot level. All this ore was milled at the St. Paul mine, about a mile west of the Billy Sunday. The shaft is near the north end line of the claim.

In 1931 the headframe had been removed. A small gasoline-driven hoist and compressor run by separate gas engines were still in the hoist house, but as the mine had not been in operation since 1923 the equipment was not in good condition.

The main shaft is an incline which was driven on the vein that strikes N. 5°–10° W. and dips about 45° E. near the surface but steepens to about 60° at 70 feet below the surface. Drifts have been turned off from this shaft at the 25, 60, and 120-foot levels. (See fig. 22.) The shaft continues below the 120-foot level, but water stands about 30 feet below the floor. On the 120-foot level there is an 80-foot crosscut eastward, at the end of which there are short drifts north and south and a winze on the vein in which water stands 30 feet below the level of the crosscut. The timbers are in fair condition throughout, but many of the underground openings have been partly filled by the crushed vein material that has fallen from the walls.

The short north drift on the 25-foot level could be entered for only 50 feet, as it contained much ice, as did the open stopes above and below it. The vein, as shown by pillars, averaged 3 feet in width and consisted of 12 to 14 inches of quartz beneath the hanging-wall slip, the remainder of the vein filling being crushed schist and quartz. The whole vein assayed about 80 cents to the ton, as shown by a sample cut across a pillar 30 feet north of the shaft.

On the 60-foot level the north drift is caved just beyond the shaft. It is reported that the stopes go through to the surface and to the 120-foot level for a length of about 75 feet. In the south drift, which was open to the face a distance of 150 feet, the vein strikes north and dips 60° E. It varies in width from 1 to 5 feet and includes crushed schist and quartz. Stopes have been carried through to the surface and to the level below in an area near the shaft. About 20 feet south of the shaft a crosscut to the west intersects another vein 40 feet below the main Billy Sunday vein. This west vein, called the Rat Hole vein, probably because of the very small dimensions of the crosscut, strikes N. 10° E. and dips 80° E. A small stope has been carried up on the vein over a length of about 60 feet. The vein is from 12 to 14 inches wide and consists largely of crushed quartz with some schist. Next to the east wall there is from 2 to 4 inches of quartz, a sample of which assayed $24.58 a ton. The quartzite schist exposed in the crosscut for about 10 feet on each side of this vein has some quartz veinlets, and this metal contact was said to be high enough to repay mining. A sample across 20 feet of the schist, but excluding the vein, gave assay results of 23 cents to the ton.

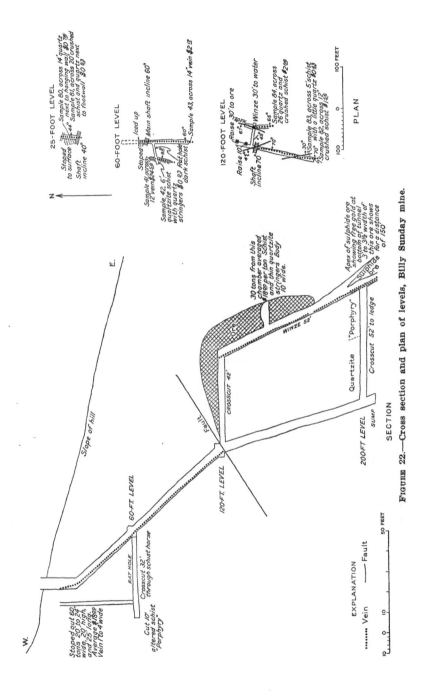

FIGURE 22.—Cross section and plan of levels, Billy Sunday mine.

On the 120-foot level the vein was cut off by a fault that strikes N. 20° W. and dips 45° W. On the level north of the shaft the vein is exposed in raises through the fault. There is a short segment of the vein exposed for 100 feet in the south drift, but it is cut off by a fault striking N. 10° E. and dipping 15°–30° E. In the face of the drift there is a fracture zone that consists of 5 feet of crushed sheared schist containing very little quartz. Samples from this place assayed from 83 cents to $1.56 a ton.

Ten feet north of the shaft, below the fault, a crosscut was run eastward for 50 feet through schists to a vein that was thought to correspond to the Billy Sunday above the 120-foot level, and from this crosscut short drifts were run both north and south. The south drift was started along a 12 to 14 inch fault zone of ground-up schist and clay that strikes N. 20° E. and dips 67° W. and then follows a vein that dips 65° E. and strikes due north. This vein is from 8 to 24 inches wide and consists mainly of quartz but contains also some crushed schist. At the face of the drift 50 feet south of the crosscut there is 12 inches of crushed schist above the footwall slip and 14 inches of quartz next the hanging wall slip, a sample of which assayed $2.06 to the ton. At the crosscut a winze, which was sunk on the vein, is said to go down to the 200-foot level but was under water 30 feet below the drift. Just above the water level in a drift which extends south of the winze for about 25 feet there is a well-defined quartz vein 4 to 10 inches wide. Mr. Smith, who managed the property at the time this level was driven, stated that in this winze at the 200-foot level the vein was 5 feet wide and occurred between well-defined walls and that samples, taken both by himself and by a representative of the Alaska Agricultural College and School of Mines, assayed from $54 to $250 a ton. Some samples of ore said to have come from the 200-foot level are of remarkably high grade and show free gold with stibnite and arsenopyrite in both white quartz and in quartzite schist.

In 1931 at the Billy Sunday mine no ore was actually blocked out in the engineering sense. It is possible that the vein exposed in the east drift on the 120-foot level and in the winze may not be the same as that developed by the upper levels of the mine, but not enough ground is accessible for study to make it possible to determine that fact.

MOHAWK

The Mohawk mine (no. 23, fig. 18) is on the upper part of St. Patrick Creek on the east side of Ester Dome, about 12½ miles by a good automobile road west of Fairbanks. The group consists of eight full claims and a fractional claim, all of which were surveyed for patent in October 1925, under mineral survey 1922. The claims are the Bondholder, Bondholder Extension, Peg Leg, Yellow Jacket, Mohawk No. 3, Mohawk, Liberty, Mohawk No. 2, and Spite Fraction. This group of claims is the property of Joseph Henderson and John McGinn.

The property is reported to have produced over $200,000, most of which has been taken out since 1925 under the personal direction of Mr. Henderson. Practically all of the output has come from ore taken from the Mohawk vein, in the southern part of the group of claims, though there has also been a little production from the Bondholder vein, in the northern part of the group. Near the mouth of the lower tunnel, at an elevation of about 900 feet on the south side of St. Patrick Creek, there is an 8-foot Chile mill of the Lane type driven by a semi-Diesel engine which also drives a 7 by 9 inch jaw-crusher of the Blake type. The mill, prior to 1931, was driven by steam generated by wood and coal. It is said that the cost of power was reduced 80 percent by the change to the internal-combustion type of engine. The mill is well housed, but as its water supply is obtained from the lower tunnel, which has been dammed near the portal, it has not been operated during the winter. Near the portal of the main tunnel, at an elevation of 1,000 feet, there is a small compressor run by a Fordson tractor.

The main workings are on the Mohawk vein, which, in general, strikes N. 30° E. and dips 40°–70° ESE., with an average dip of about 60°. They comprise 3 adit tunnels and 2 intermediate levels between the middle or main tunnel and the upper tunnel. The underground work includes over 2,900 feet of drifts and 1,800 feet of raises and winzes and has developed the vein over a total length of 1,300 feet and to a vertical depth of 232 feet at the face of the main tunnel. (See pl. 10.)

At the time the mine was visited in 1931, the upper tunnel was half full of ice and caved just beyond the split, at a point before the ore bodies were reached. That portion of the tunnel which was accessible had been driven through nearly flat-lying biotite-quartz schist. The lowest tunnel just above the level of the mill was flooded by a dam near the mouth and was used as a mill-water reservoir.

The main tunnel was open to the face, but the crosscuts and drifts on faults both to the east and west of it were caved and inaccessible. The main adit is about 1,400 feet long and follows the vein all the way. Practically all ore has been stoped above this level to the surface for the first 900 feet of the tunnel. There are stopes below this level for the first 320 feet, or to a point at the south end of the split in the vein. (See pl. 10.)

The fault zone near the mouth of the tunnel is nearly 50 feet wide and has a general trend of N. 30° W., though the footwall slip strikes N. 10° W. and dips 45° W. and the south or hanging-wall slip strikes N. 56° W. and dips 30° S. The ground between these two slips is very heavy and is tightly timbered and lagged. South of this fault the vein is practically continuous for 1,000 feet, though a little south of this fault it is offset about 10 feet by a north-south zone of movement that dips 45° W. South of this zone the vein splits, inclosing a horse of schist about 130 feet long. The ore on both sides of the horse has been mined, and the open caved stopes continue on the vein southward for 360 feet to raise 10. In this raise the ore was cut off 60 feet above the tunnel level by a flat fault.

About 40 feet south of raise 10 a N. 35° W. fault dipping 40°–50° NE. cuts across the vein. The apparent movement on this fault was normal, and the vein is displaced about 10 feet. The slickensides on various slip planes in this fault zone indicate nearly horizontal movement.

The vein south of this fault has been followed 300 feet to the face of the main tunnel, where it disappears against a fault that strikes N. 20° E. and dips 40° W. In the various stopes on this level where the width can be seen and judged from pillars and openings, the vein ranged in width from 9 inches to 6 feet and averaged a little over 3 feet throughout. The ore yielded from $15 to $35 a ton and according to Mr. Henderson averaged more than $20 a ton for all the ore mined above the main tunnel level.

The chief area under development in the Mohawk mine in 1931 was the block of ground being opened for stoping in the two intermediate levels above the main tunnel. This ground was reached through raise 12, which rises 180 feet from a point near the face of the tunnel, and thence through a shaft from the surface, which is also used as a timber and airway.

Raise 12 followed the vein for 20 feet to a place where the vein is said to be cut off by a nearly flat eastward-dipping fault. The raise was tightly lagged, so that the fault could not now be seen. The top of the raise, 63 feet above the tunnel at the lower intermediate level, is in quartz-mica schist lying essentially horizontal. A crosscut 80 feet to the west through unaltered biotite schist connects with the drift on the vein, which has been followed for about 60 feet north and 250 feet south of the crosscut. Ore shoots and raises have been cut at 40-foot intervals, and the ore between this level and the upper intermediate level has been blocked out. This vein ranges between 2 to 4 inches of quartz near the crosscut and 6 feet of crushed schist, quartz, and gouge near the central part of the drift. At the face there is about 18 inches of crushed schist and quartz which pans well. The ore taken from the raises has been milled as soon as it was mined and has yielded from $8 to $12 a ton on the plates.

At the west end of the crosscut raise 12 on the vein connects with the upper intermediate level. The raise slopes to the east at about 45° (see pl. 10), flattening as it goes up along a fault zone about 32 feet above the lower intermediate level. There is some ore that has been dragged along the fault which was followed by the raise for about 100 feet at an inclination of about 20°. This fault is about parallel to the schistosity of the inclosing biotite-quartz schists. Above the fault the vein was picked up with almost no displacement and followed through to the upper intermediate level at an elevation of 1,128 feet, or 65 feet above the lower intermediate level and 128 feet above the lower tunnel. At the top of the drift above raise 12 on the upper intermediate level the vein is cut off by another flat fault. This fault is rather inconspicuous, consisting of 2 to 4 inches of crushed schist and gouge. It strikes N. 15° W. and dips 30° E. The segment of vein above this fault is apparently shifted about 48 feet to the east, where it has been intercepted by the east drift on the upper intermediate level.

There are apparently two veins developed in the upper intermediate level. The west vein is followed by a drift to the south for 220 feet and is connected with the lower intermediate level by winzes which show the vein continuously. Ore chutes and raises have been driven above the level, and near the face of the drift a raise had been driven 60 feet and was to be put through to the surface for air. The vein, as exposed in this drift, is from 2 to 6 feet wide and averages 4 feet. There is a well-defined quartz vein next to the hanging wall slip, but it as well as the schist between the hanging and foot wall slips is badly crushed. In places there are bunches of stibnite in the quartz vein, but they are scarce and their distribution in the vein is erratic. A fault striking north and dipping 35° E. cuts across the vein about 76 feet south of raise 12 but does not offset the vein more than 4 feet.

Eastward from the top of raise 12 a crosscut 60 feet long has been driven to the east vein, which strikes N. 20° E. and dips 62°–65° E. This vein has been followed north for at least 240 feet, and all the ore above it has been stoped to the surface. It is said that in this drift the vein north of the crosscut was cut off by a nearly flat eastward-dipping fault, but the writer was unable to verify this statement. South of the crosscut the vein has been followed for 130 feet. At a point about 90 feet south of the crosscut the vein swings to the east along a fault that strikes north and dips 50° E. The vein, however, continues through the fault, as is clearly shown in the south end of the drift.

These two veins are 60 feet apart at the line of raise 12, but are 82 feet apart 100 feet to the south, as is shown by a crosscut which follows a small east-west fracture that connects the two. This fracture is in places slightly mineralized, as is shown in a small stope about midway between the two veins.

With the exception of a few pillars of ore left in the old workings the Mohawk vein has been stoped in most of the area developed as far as raise 12. Ore carrying less than $15 to the ton was left in the mine as unprofitable when milling was done with steam power. Mr. Henderson, however, states that with the cheaper power from the semi-Diesel engine he believes it will be possible to mine and mill $8 ore at a profit and that later that limit can be reduced to $5. It is estimated that the block of ground opened from the lower intermediate level to the surface south of raise 12 contains approximately 8,300 tons of ore actually blocked out that has a value of $100,000.

What is believed to be the Mohawk vein has been opened by several shafts and pits on the north side of St. Patrick Creek, but not much development work has been done in that part of the property.

The Bondholder vein (no. 26, fig. 18), at the head of St. Patrick Creek at an elevation of 1,250 feet, is at the north end of the Mohawk group and has been opened by at least two shafts and several pits, all of which are now inaccessible. During 1930 a Mr. Hightower had a lease on a small part of the vein about 200 feet north of one of these old shafts. He installed a small hoist operated by a Ford automobile engine and extracted about 100 tons of ore above a depth of 50 feet. The vein as exposed in this opening was 4½ feet wide and contained iron and arsenic-stained quartz, a sample of which assayed $10.29 to the ton. The vein, which strikes N. 24° E. and dips 45° NW., cuts mica-quartz schist. In the midsummer of 1931 the owner of the property started another shaft about 60 feet north of Hightower's work and by mid-September had sunk it to a depth of 15 feet where the vein was 7 feet wide. About 400 tons of ore extracted in sinking this shaft had been milled and yielded over $10 a ton. There is little sulphide left in this surface ore, but occasionally both arsenopyrite and stibnite are found in the less fractured rock.

The owner states that in a 142-foot shaft about 150 feet north of his present work the vein averages 6 feet in width. Estimated on that basis the block of ground between Hightower's 50-foot shaft and this deep shaft should contain about 7,400 tons of $10 ore that can be mined profitably.

The Bondholder vein has been traced both north and south by surface pits for several hundred feet and seems to be well mineralized throughout.

The crosscut tunnel, which was started at an elevation of 1,100 feet on St. Patrick Creek to develop the Bondholder vein, was

caved at the mouth. The **tunnel** is driven in a N. 20° W. direction
and is said to be between 600 and 700 feet long but did not reach
the vein. The dump is practically all biotite-quartz schist.

By the middle of September 1931 a new road, built to haul ore
from the Bondholder mine, had just been completed around the
south side of St. Patrick Creek to the Mohawk mill. There are at
least four veins exposed in cuts along this road. At two other places
on Mohawk ground there are prospects where more work will probably result in the discovery of other veins.

WANDERING JEW

The workings on the Wandering Jew claim (no. 24, fig. 18), the
property of Joseph H. McDonald, of Berry post office, lie in the
saddle between St. Patrick and Eva Creeks at an elevation of 1,425
feet, about five eighths of a mile west of the Mohawk mine and 2
miles north of Ester. There is no equipment at the mine; all work
including hoisting was done by hand. The latest work on this
ground was done in the winter of 1930–31 by lessees, among whom
were William McConn and William McCann, who took out 75 tons
of $21 ore and 45 tons of $10 ore. This ore was recovered above a
depth of 50 feet and in a stope about 50 feet long.

The vein, which strikes north and dips 75°–80° E., is from 4 to 18
inches wide and consists of white quartz that in places contains some
sulphides. It is not so much crushed as some of the other veins but
is stained with patches of iron and arsenic oxides. A sample taken
in two cuts, one 4 inches and one 12 inches across the vein on the
30-foot level, assayed $25.35 a ton.

The shaft is practically vertical and 50 feet deep. A drift at the
30-foot level was driven south for 50 feet to a fault that strikes east
and dips 37° N. The fault is marked by 4 inches of gouge, but it
has not displaced the vein, which has been stoped from the surface
to this level for 20 feet south of the shaft. In the north drift on
the 30-foot level a fault that strikes N. 30° W. and dips 35°–40° NE.
cuts off the vein about 25 feet north of the shaft. All the ore up to
the fault has been mined out, but the vein was not traced to the
north of the fault.

The vein has been traced on the surface by pits for about 400 feet
south of the shaft, but as none of the ore found there panned well no
additional sinking was attempted. North of the shaft the vein had
not been traced beyond the fault.

FIRST CHANCE

The First Chance mine (no. 25, fig. 18) lies just north of the Wandering Jew mine, on the head of St. Patrick Creek at an elevation of

1,325 feet. Sam Stay owns a half interest in this claim and Mc-Laughlin and Franklin each own a quarter interest. It has produced $26,000 from 520 tons of ore. All the information on such of the workings as were in such condition that they could not be examined at the time of visit was given by Mr. Stay. The shaft is 120 feet deep, and all the ore above the 100-foot level to a fault 70 feet north of the shaft has been stoped. South of the shaft the ore was of somewhat lower grade, averaging less than $20 a ton below the 100-foot level. South of the shaft the ore was stoped from the surface to a depth of 70 feet. The vein ranged from 6 inches to 4 feet in width but averaged about 12 inches throughout the stoped area. The richest ore was found where the vein was narrow.

The vein as seen on the surface strikes N. 10° E. and dips 44° W. The inclined shaft was iced up 20 feet below the collar. A crosscut tunnel in the gulch to the north and 100 feet below the collar of the shaft was driven S. 70° W. but is now caved 75 feet from the mouth. The accessible portion is entirely in schists that strike north and dip 16°–20° E.

PROMETHEUS

The Prometheus shaft (no. 27, fig. 18), at an elevation of 1,500 feet, is close to the trail that leads from the divide near the Wandering Jew to the monument on the summit of Ester Dome. The lower part of the shaft was filled with water and could not be examined. It is reported to be 60 feet deep, and drifts had evidently been started at the bottom.

The vein apparently strikes N. 40° E., but it was not possible to determine the dip from the surface exposures. On the dump at this place is about 60 tons of ore consisting of white quartz cut by later veinlets of gray quartz with sulphides. A grab sample from the ore pile assayed $9.52 a ton in gold and silver. The sample is one of the few taken in the district which showed noteworthy amounts of silver. It contained 6.40 ounces of silver to the ton. A polished section of a specimen of this ore, rich in sulphides, shows arsenopyrite, jamesonite, and covellite. It is reported that the vein is 8 feet wide.

BIG BLUE

The Big Blue lead (no. 28, fig. 18) is exposed in a number of shallow shafts and pits at an elevation of 1,550 feet on the trail a short distance west of the Prometheus shaft. The vein strikes N. 27° E., but its dip could not be determined from the exposures in the caved pits. Apparently the lode is wide, and the dumps indicate that it occupies a faulted zone with much crushed schist, quartz, and gouge. The country rock is mainly biotite schist, but there are many pieces of quartz-mica schist on several of the dumps.

MICHLEY

The Michley prospects, at the head of Sheep Creek (no. 29, fig. 18), are at an elevation of 1,500 feet and about 100 feet above the creek level. The main development is a 200-foot crosscut tunnel that has been driven S. 75° E. into the hill through flat-lying quartz-mica schist. Several narrow quartz veinlets with north-south strikes and steep dips to either the east or the west are exposed in the tunnel. At a point 155 feet from the mouth of the tunnel there are short drifts to both north and south on a vein that strikes N. 4° W. and dips 60° E. near the crosscut but is nearly vertical at the face of the south drift. The vein ranges from 2 inches of white quartz to a zone with 12 inches of quartz between 4 to 6 inches of gouge on the walls. The ore from a small stope just north of the crosscut is said to have milled about $10 a ton. The quartz is milky white, is not badly crushed, and does not appear to carry much sulphide or to be well mineralized.

About 50 feet above the lower tunnel there is a 50-foot tunnel on the vein that is exposed near the face of the crosscut. The vein has been traced both north and south by shallow pits for several hundred feet.

SANFORD

On the summit of the ridge between Sheep and Happy Creeks (no. 30, fig. 18), at an elevation of about 1,550 feet, is a group of six claims held by J. H. Sanford. The main underground development is a shaft that is 2 miles in an air line northeast of the summit of Ester Dome and about 18 miles by road northwest of Fairbanks. About 150 tons of ore that yielded $6,700 has been milled from this property. Part of this ore is said to have averaged $52 a ton. No low-grade ore has been milled, as there is no reduction plant at the mine, and the haulage charge to the Mohawk mill is high. There is no equipment at the mine other than a hand windlass and black-smith tools.

The shaft, which is 105 feet deep, was sunk on the dip of the vein, which strikes N. 40° E. and dips 45° SE. From the surface to a depth of 20 feet the vein has been stoped both north and south of the shaft. From the shaft there is a 65-foot drift south at the 20-foot level and a 60-foot drift south on the 65-foot level. All ore above the 65-foot level has been stoped and below it the vein pinches to a 2-inch seam of gouge and 10 to 12 inches of quartz of low tenor. At the bottom of the shaft is a vertical vein which joins the vein in the shaft and strikes N. 20° E. This vertical vein has been opened on the surface by several pits now caved, about 30 feet east of the main shaft. It is said to have carried some high-grade ore.

ELMES

The property of the Elmes Gold Mining Co. (no. 31, fig. 18) embraces part of the valley of Happy Creek, and the mill is on the south side of the creek about a mile northeast of the Mohawk mill. The mill was formerly the custom mill at Chena. The claims have been in litigation and are now held by Mr. Nickaloff. They extend southwestward up the ridge from the mill and have been opened by a tunnel and a shaft at an elevation of 1,250 feet. As a result of caving both these workings were inaccessible in June 1931, and the mill building was locked. It is said that the jaw crusher and 5 of the original 10 stamps were put in place and were run by steam power.

To judge from surface exposures the vein strikes about N. 25°–30° E. The shaft is said to be 100 feet deep, and the size of the dump indicates that the tunnel, which is about 50 feet lower, must be several hundred feet long. The rock on the dump is mica schist and carries considerable vein quartz. The ore remaining in the bin at the tunnel is crushed quartz, gouge, and schist, a grab sample of which assayed $8.64 a ton.

GRANT

The property of O. M. Grant (no. 32, fig. 18) is situated on the point of the ridge north of St. Patrick Creek and about a mile northeast of the Mohawk mill. The shaft is at an elevation of 900 feet and about one eighth of a mile east of the road leading from the Mohawk to the Elmes mine. The shaft was originally started for the purpose of reaching a buried gravel channel and was sunk through muck and gravel to bedrock, which was found dipping east at a steep angle. No pay gravel was found, but the top of a quartz vein was struck, and the shaft was continued down on the vein to a total depth of 240 feet. The plan of the workings (see fig. 23) shows that the two drifts at the 200-foot and 240 foot levels had been run a total distance of 280 feet. In June 1931, when the property was visited, the owners were absent and the shaft could not be entered because of bad air. There is a small steam hoist operating a dump-bucket rig such as is used at the deep-gravel placer mines. It is said that between 500 and 600 tons of ore was milled from this vein that yielded between $15 and $20 a ton. The vein is said to strike N. 40° E. and dip 65° E. and to be 5 or 6 feet wide, with 2 to 4 feet of quartz.

The ore seen on the dump was the usual crushed recemented iron and arsenic stained quartz typical of the district.

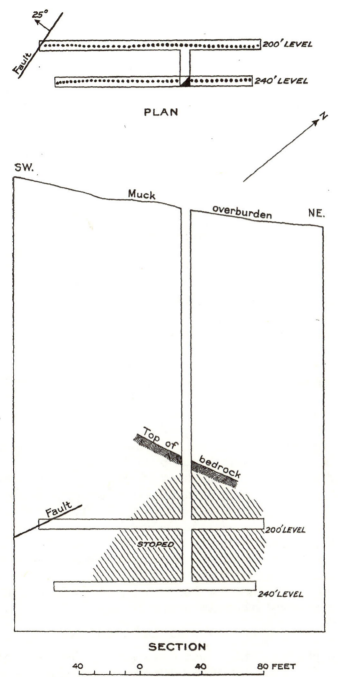

FIGURE 23.—Plan and section of workings, Grant mine.

The Clipper claims (no. 33, fig. 18) are situated on the east fork of Eva Creek and are held by Messrs. McDonald, Michley, Hess, Thomas, and McCann. The main underground development consists of a crosscut tunnel trending N. 85° E. whose portal stands at an elevation of 1,100 feet. The tunnel is 237 feet long and cuts through biotite schist with some layers of quartzite, the bedding and schistosity of which are parallel and dip 10°–15° NNE. Several narrow fissures are cut by the tunnel, but only one near the mouth shows any amount of mineralization. It strikes N. 20° W., dips 85° W., and is from 1 inch to 8 inches wide. It carries a little sulphide and free gold and is said to assay about $12 a ton.

MISCELLANEOUS PROSPECTS ON ESTER DOME

Several claims owned by H. N. Macomb lie between the Mohawk and Grant mines on the north side of St. Patrick Creek. The chief development is in two shafts 30 and 50 feet deep on a vein that strikes northeast and dips 60° SE. This work was caved and inaccessible, but the ore seen on the dump consisted of crushed schist, gouge, and quartz.

Helbarth Lepsoe has two quartz claims on the ridge east of Nugget Gulch at an elevation of 1,600 to 1,800 feet on a white quartz vein about 20 feet wide that strikes N. 40° W. and parallels a dike of granite porphyry. These claims are about 1½ miles northwest of the Grant mine (no. 2, fig. 18). Only a small amount of prospecting and development has been done on these claims.

At an elevation of 1,300 feet on the ridge between Ready Bullion and Eva Creeks there are some shallow trenches on a vein that strikes N. 35° E. and carries some promising ore.

The Merian claim lies southeast of the Ryan group, near the head of Ace Creek. A long tunnel was driven by J. W. Bigelow northward through schists that dip 15°–16° E. This tunnel is caved at a point about 75 feet north of the portal.

The Flower claim, owned by William McCann and Mrs. Olsen, is on the point between the two forks of Eva Creek at an elevation of 1,200 feet, a short distance east of the St. Paul mill. There are several shallow shafts and a short tunnel (which was caved in June 1931) on a vertical vein that strikes N. 10° E.

MISCELLANEOUS GOLD-LODE PROSPECTS

A few properties visited during this investigation are in neither the Ester Dome nor the Pedro Dome area as defined in this report. The fact that prospects have been found in widely scattered localities outside of the main metallized areas indicates the need for more detailed prospecting throughout the district. As will be noted, most of the scattered prospects described in the following pages are far removed from large masses of intrusive rocks.

RIDGE

On the ridge south of Engineer Creek, at an elevation of 1,450 feet and about 2¼ miles in an air line southeast of the highway bridge over Engineer Creek, Frank Isaacson has a prospect called the Ridge claim. The location was made December 14, 1930. Two shafts have been sunk about 15 feet on a vein that strikes N. 50° E. and dips south. In July 1931 these shafts were without ladders and had water in them. The vein appears to be about 14 inches wide. A grab sample from a pile of about 10 tons of ore on the dump assayed $15.96 a ton.

ENGINEER

On the point of the ridge about one eighth of a mile south of the bridge over Engineer Creek on the highway there are a few prospect pits on two parallel veins that appear to strike N. 70° E. The work is all badly caved, so that little can be seen of the veins in place. A little ore at one of the open cuts is the usual iron-stained white quartz carrying arsenopyrite. A grab sample of this ore assayed $2.86 a ton.

PETERSON

Near the benchmark on the knob between Goldstream and Engineer Creeks at an elevation of 1,600 feet, about 2 miles in an air line southeast of Fox, James Peterson is working on some prospects. Most of the holes are in barren schist or have not penetrated the dirt overburden. One row of holes, however, is apparently close to a vein, for promising float occurred in the surface material.

BUNKER HILL

Albert Goodwin has some prospects on the divide north of Big Eldorado Creek about 2½ miles west of the divide where the Fox-Dome road crosses from the Goldstream to the Chatanika drainage basin. (See pl. 3.) These prospects are near the road leading to the Eagle Antimony mine and are 300 feet west of the quarter corner on the line between secs. 14 and 23, T. 2 N., R. 1 W.

A crosscut tunnel now caved is about 75 feet vertically below the summit of the ridge and runs north, crosscutting a zone of brecciated iron-stained schist that strikes N. 70° E. and stands vertical. This zone is 50 feet wide, as is shown by several open cuts and pits. The material on the dumps is all more or less iron-stained and contains vein quartz. A grab sample taken from various dumps, in the attempt to determine the average value of this zone, assayed only 23 cents to the ton.

About a quarter of a mile west-northwest of the tunnel, on the crest of the ridge, there is a shaft said to be 102 feet deep on a vein that strikes N. 15° W. and dips 70° E. The timbers of this shaft were gone just below the collar, so it could not be examined in detail. The material on the dump is mica schist, representing the hanging wall, and a blocky quartz-mica schist which Mr. Goodwin says forms the footwall. He states that the vein averaged 12 inches in width at the surface but was only 2 inches wide at a depth of 50 feet. There are said to be short drifts on the 25 and 60 foot levels. It is reported that 8 tons of ore taken out above the 25-foot level milled 13 ounces of gold. A grab sample of a small pile of ore left on the dump assayed $24.06 to the ton.

JANIKSELA

John Janiksela has a claim on the north side of Goldstream Creek, about 1½ miles east-northeast of Fox. There are two shafts on the ledge, which strikes east; one was caved and the other was under water, so that no examination was possible. Apparently the lode follows the contact of mica schist and a black graphite schist. The material in the ore pile was a mixture of quartz, feldspar, and coarse-grained mica more nearly resembling pegmatite than vein quartz. It is said that some cassiterite (tin ore) was found here, but none was noted in the material on the dump.

PERRAULT

The workings of the Perrault property are in the saddle at the divide between Pearl Creek, a tributary of Fish Creek, and Smallwood Creek, about 8 miles by trail east of Gilmore post office, on the Steese Highway. No work was in progress in July 1931, when this area was visited, and all the openings were either caved or iced up. The several shafts and a tunnel on Pearl Creek all seem to be on the same lead, which apparently strikes N. 50° E. The vein material seen on the dumps is different from most of the quartz seen in the district. It consists of a breccia of schist fragments partly cemented by white quartz. The spaces between fragments are not all completely filled, and the quartz crystals have grown out from the wall into open vugs. Very little sulphide was noted in the ore piles at any of the shafts. This property was visited in 1912 by Smith,[47] who reports that the shaft at that time was 50 feet deep and had yielded several tons of $24 ore. On the adjoining claim to the south he also reports a 38-foot shaft from which 20 tons of $25 ore had been mined.

[47] Smith, P. S., op. cit. (Bull. 525), p. 166.

EGAN

J. J. and Dan Egan have located a small group of claims on the point of the ridge between Jack Creek and Martin Creek, in the head of Kokomo Creek Basin, about 1½ miles north of Coffee Dome at an elevation of 500 feet. (See pl. 3.) Several shallow pits and trenches dug during 1930 and 1931 have indicated the presence of 4 or 5 different veins apparently spaced about 100 feet apart. They strike N. 40° W. and dip 45°–60° SW. The country rock is a silvery biotite schist that lies nearly flat or has a low dip to the south. One of the lodes is a crushed zone of schist and quartz about 8 feet wide. Most of the veins are from 1 to 2 feet wide. A sample across one of the veins 20 inches wide assayed $7.38 a ton. The mineralization is typical of the Fairbanks district ores and indicates that further prospecting is warranted.

BIRCH HILL

In a small quarry opened for road metal at the point of Birch Hill, about 2 miles northeast of Fairbanks, two veins are exposed, cutting schist. They strike N. 50° E. and dip 62° SE. One vein is 18 inches between walls, of which 6 inches consists of crushed schist and gouge next the footwall and the remainder of crushed quartz. It carries no values.

About 10 feet west of the vein mentioned above there is an 8-inch vein of bluish-white quartz, very glassy but with specks of limonite, which appear to be casts of pyrite crystals. This vein showed no value on assay.

About 60 feet east of the quarry some work had been done on a 28-inch ledge of quartz that strikes N. 70° W. The vein splits and reunites and is somewhat crushed and iron-stained in places, but nowhere does it resemble the mineralized veins of the district. A sample cut across 28 inches showed no value on assay.

LEIDY

The Steve Leidy claims, on the north side of Gilmore Creek, are about a quarter of a mile west of the mouth of Tom Creek, beside the road. A shaft has been sunk at least 40 feet on a vein of glassy quartz that strikes N. 70° W. and dips 50° N. The surface schists have been ground-sluiced, and it seems likely that the quartz is barren and that what gold was found in the vein near the surface was placer gold. There is a thin covering of placer gravel on the schist bench in which this work was done.

BILLY

The Billy group of three claims is in the Kokomo Creek Basin about 2 miles east-northeast of Coffee Dome, just east of the limits of the area shown on plate 3. The claims cover a ledge of barren white quartz that strikes N. 20° W. and dips 70° W. across the strike of the schistosity. The ledge is 20 feet wide, and shearing on the edges has produced a rough sheeting of the quartz. No sulphides were seen in the quartz, and none of the usual second and third generations of quartz was noted. Sulphides were absent. A little iron stain on the joint planes near the edges of this ledge was probably derived from alteration of the femic minerals in the enclosing schist. Samples of the more highly iron-stained quartz assayed 29 cents to the ton.

ANTIMONY DEPOSITS

The Fairbanks district is a potential source of high-grade antimony ore, principally stibnite. The deposits are, however, so far from markets that they can be worked at a profit only when the price for the metal is unusually high. They were worked during the World War period but have been idle ever since except for a short time in 1926.

Most of the development workings on deposits valuable mainly for their antimony content were inaccessible in 1931. The writer was therefore unable to study the antimony lodes as a whole, but during his study of the gold lodes he obtained some information in regard to antimony deposits that is here recorded. The antimony deposits of Alaska were described in detail by Brooks [48] in 1916, and his report still remains the standard reference work on that subject. The scattered observations here recorded give what information is available concerning developments on the antimony lodes since Brooks' report was issued and are intended only to supplement it.

SCRAFFORD

The Scrafford property, on Eagle Creek, a southwesterly tributary of Treasure Creek, was described in detail by Brooks. [49] When visited in August 1931 all the workings at the mine were inaccessible. It was reported that the last work done was in 1926 by R. C. Woods, who drove the main tunnel in 300 feet and shipped a total of about 1,500 tons of sorted ore. The vein in places is said to have been as much as 15 feet wide between walls, with here and there 9 feet of solid stibnite.

There is a considerable accumulation of mixed ore and screened waste still on the dumps. Apparently this material could be concentrated by jigging to yield a marketable product if the price of antimony should warrant reopening this mine. Samples of various

---

[48] Brooks, A. H., Antimony deposits of Alaska: U.S. Geol. Survey Bull. 649, pp. 17–41, 1916.
[49] Idem, pp. 28–29.

types of ore on the dump indicate that the gold and silver in the ore probably does not exceed $2.43 a ton even in those parts where the vein consists of a mixture of iron-stained quartz and stibnite.

EAGLE CREEK

Some claims east of Eagle Creek, in the Treasure Creek Basin, have been located by Al Goodwin, of Fairbanks. Mr. Goodwin shipped some stibnite from this ground in 1926 from an 85-foot inclined shaft and a 60-foot tunnel. He reports that the tunnel crosscut 48 feet of crushed sheared schist in which the stibnite occurred as lenses. The earlier work is now caved, but the material on the dump is a black crushed schist with considerable pyrite, largely altered to sulphur from its long exposure to the air. This ore zone strikes N. 80° E. and dips 45° S. It is clearly on the same zone of fissuring as the Scrafford property described above and has been opened by a short tunnel and shaft in Independence Gulch, a mile farther east.

M'QUEEN

All the workings on the McQueen property (no. 4, fig. 18), located on the ridge about a quarter of a mile west of Ester Dome, were caved in June 1931. There were evidently two shafts and either a tunnel or a level not far below the surface. This work indicated that the vein had a strike of N. 30° E. and a rather steep eastward dip. It is said that over 100 tons of stibnite ore was shipped from this place during the period of high prices in 1916 to 1918.

TUNGSTEN DEPOSITS

During the World War tungsten minerals commanded very high prices, and under the stimulus of this unusual demand several properties in the Fairbanks district that contained tungsten minerals were rapidly developed (see fig. 24), and some ore was shipped. These properties were visited in 1916 by Mertie,[50] who described the deposits and their development. At the end of the war tungsten prices declined abruptly, and the mines became inactive. It seems doubtful that these deposits can be profitably worked under any but abnormal conditions of price for tungsten minerals.

The only tungsten property on which development work was in progress in 1931 was the Stepovich ground, at the head of Yellow Creek, a tributary of Fish Creek, where some prospecting was done.

To summarize, it may be said that in the Fairbanks district some of the tungsten minerals occur as disseminated deposits in mineralized zones or ore shoots in the country rock, but in other places they

---

[50] Mertie, J. B., Jr., Lode mining in the Fairbanks district, Alaska, in 1916: U.S. Geol. Survey Bull. 662, pp. 418–423, 1918.

occur as distinct veins and stringers. In some deposits the tungsten-bearing solutions have clearly been derived from near-by granitic intrusives, but in other places such a connection is remote and not demonstrable, and the tungsten minerals occur in quartz veins comparable with and even identical with those carrying gold ores. The fact that some of these tungsten-bearing deposits appear to lie in or in close proximity to lenses of limestone in the schist has been interpreted by some as indicating that they had been formed principally through processes of replacement, but this conclusion does not appear to be supported by the field evidence afforded by other deposits. From what is now known regarding the occurrence of tungsten

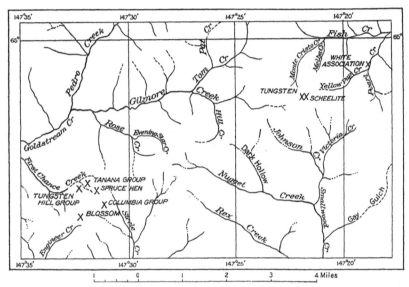

FIGURE 24.—Sketch map showing tungsten lode claims in the Fairbanks district.

minerals in this region it may be said that the geologic conditions throughout a considerable part of the area adjacent to Fairbanks appear to be favorable for the formation of deposits of this type, but that search for such places is not regarded as likely to be profitable, owing to the sporadic occurrence, the high cost of development, and the present relatively low price paid for the product.

FUTURE OF LODE MINING

The gold-bearing lodes of the Fairbanks district have been fairly well prospected on the surface in some places, but much ground remains to be prospected more thoroughly. Very few properties are actually developed. The few producing mines could greatly expand their yield with more adequate finances for development and equipment and with more technically proficient direction. There are 6 or 8 regular producers now, and it is believed that there are at least 20 and possibly 50 properties which might furnish an average of not less than 50 tons of ore a day each, and possibly a dozen of them might supply an average of 100 tons a day. The average tenor of ore from these mines could probably be maintained at not less than $10 a ton, and for considerable periods of time some of them might average as high as $15 a ton. On this basis it does not seem at all unwarranted to suggest that after they had been properly opened the gold-lode mines of the district might produce ore worth several million dollars a year for many years.

INDEX

161

This original publication came with additional plates and/or maps included in the document or the back pocket of the publication. Miningbooks.com has digitally scanned and formatted these plates and/or maps and put them on a CD ROM. Due to the printing and distribution process we use, some of our distributors and retailers may not have the capability to add this CD in with their drop-ship process. If you did not receive this CD Rom with your book we have made this CD available directly from our website www.miningbooks.com for you to purchase at a nominal cost in order to cover shipping , handling, and materials.